The Art of Trend Trading

The Art of Trend Trading

ANIMAL SPIRITS AND YOUR
PATH TO PROFITS

Michael Parness

WILEY

Published by John Wiley & Sons, Inc., Hoboken, New Jersey.
Published simultaneously in Canada.

For general information on our other products and services or for technical support, please contact our Customer Care Department within the United States at (800) 762-2974, outside the United States at (317) 572-3993 or fax (317) 572-4002.

Wiley publishes in a variety of print and electronic formats and by print-on-demand. Some material included with standard print versions of this book may not be included in e-books or in print-on-demand. If this book refers to media such as a CD or DVD that is not included in the version you purchased, you may download this material at http://booksupport.wiley.com. For more information about Wiley products, visit www.wiley.com.

Library of Congress Cataloging-in-Publication Data:

Names: Parness, Michael, author.
Title: The art of trend trading : animal spirits and your path to profits / Michael Parness.
Description: Hoboken, New Jersey : John Wiley & Sons, Inc., [2016] | Includes index.
Identifiers: LCCN 2015032740 (print) | LCCN 2015038538 (ebook) | ISBN 9781119028017 (cloth) | ISBN 9781119185215 (ePDF) | ISBN 9781119185321 (epub)
Subjects: LCSH: Investments. | Speculation. | Investment analysis.
Classification: LCC HG4521 .P353 2016 (print) | LCC HG4521 (ebook) | DDC 332.64–dc23
LC record available at http://lccn.loc.gov/2015032740

Cover Design: Wiley
Cover Image: Dollar Bird © iStock.com / hdoggrafix

Printed in the United States of America

10 9 8 7 6 5 4 3 2 1

Contents

Foreword

Michael Di Gioia
CEO Affinity Trading
Partner—World Series of Trading
(www.worldseriesoftrading.com)

Michael Parness and I come from very different parts of the financial world, and though very different, we are complementary in many ways. I got started in trading in the late 1990s. I had just come back from a summer in Spain and a few different study-abroad programs. While studying (partying ;-)) in Europe, I had started to trade and monitor my accounts online. When I got back to New York and started graduate school, I also started a job as a head hunter in New York City. In 1998, it did not take me long to figure out where the best-paying jobs were in NYC—Wall Street. As a head hunter, I knew that there was one company that was hiring more people than any other firm. It was an Internet online trading company. So I sent myself out for an interview there, and sure enough, I got a job offer.

So my trading experience started more from the direction of being a person on a professional trading desk. Mind you, when I got started at Precision Edge Securities (later, edgetrade.com) in 1999, I was not a licensed broker. I had to cram to pass my series 7 in January 2000. Professional trading at that time was mainly a scalping style, widely known as SOES trading, because we used systems like SOES, Select Net, and Instinet to route our orders. I traded and helped run a trading desk where there was a mix of retail brokers trading for their clients (we at the trading desk executed their orders), retail trader SOES scalping, and momentum trading. For the retail brokers, I was more like a foot soldier. I worked and executed orders, and that was my focus. It was very short term, and I had no idea why the clients or the brokers were buying or selling. My performance was measured entirely by my execution price versus

VWAP (volume-weighted average price). As for the day traders, well, I was one of them when not trading a client order.

As a licensed professional trader, I had no idea what guys like Michael Parness were looking at or basing their trade ideas off of. I was more a cog in the proverbial wheel who knew a lot about execution and short-term trading technicals. Trends to me simply meant higher highs and higher lows.

When I went to my next firm, Terra Nova Trading, Michael Parness was one of their biggest and most active trader clients. His students were also many of our clients; it was there that I started to learn about his trend trading tactics. They were very different from the very short-term execution-based concepts that I was used to on a professional trading desk.

Needless to say watching him and his trader/students pull multidollar moves from stocks and options when I would high-five the guy next to me on the trade desk if I took a trade for a point ($1), I really wanted to learn how he made such amazing picks. Fast forward a few years and Michael and I were having lunch at Broadway Joe's on 46th Street in New York City and he was telling me about his trading and a new idea, the World Series of Trading (Michael and I are now partners on the www.worldseriesoftrading.com).

Michael and I still did not get together officially for a few more years when we collaborated on "Ka-chingos in Paradise," a live trading mentorship in the Bahamas. Sadly, I have a short attention span and require visuals to learn. When Michael and I did the seminar together in the Bahamas, I finally started to get what he was talking about. His trends were statistical and event driven. In all my years of technical trading, I always knew that news trumped technicals—the problem was that I just did not know how to interpret the news catalyst events. What Michael has done is package and simplify the tradable news catalyst events into his Trend Trading System. After that seminar in the Bahamas, we both knew we wanted to merge Michael and his Trend Trading System and Affinity Trading Institute's well-established multifaceted D+TPTSP (Discipline + Trend, Pattern, Trigger, Stop and Target). Our disciplines, while different, fit perfectly together. I would always say a good swing trade would turn into two to five days of great day trading for me. Now I had a great source of additional swing trades.

Once Michael and I got together, we came up with more awesome concepts like "Day Trading Stocks for Cents and Swing Trading

Options for Dollars." In case you have not figured it out yet, I teach "Day Trading Stocks for Cents" and Michael teaches the "Swing Trading Options for Dollar-Plus Moves." What this did for my own trading is that I day trade the first few hours of the day for income and swing trade for wealth-building trades using options. My approach has now become technical plus I have learned to make money using Michael's New Catalyst Trend Trading to score larger core and swing moves.

Michael's unique approach to trading the markets is not only revolutionary, it has made the markets accessible to the average Joe. The market should be many other businesses, where anyone can try to trade and not be at a distinct disadvantage. Michael's system levels the playing field and allows people to, as he says, "Go for their own financial freedom."

I'm proud to be Michael Parness's partner with World Series of Trading (www.worldseriesoftrading.com) and Affinity Trading (www.affinitytrading.com) and to call him a great friend as well.

We both strive to help people achieve their financial goals. It's hard to find great traders; it's even harder to find great traders who are also great educators.

Michael Parness is one of the rare breed who can do both with great success.

CHAPTER 1

Wishing You a Slow Rise

At times, I feel like a victim of some of my own successes in relation to working with new, and sometimes long-term, clients. Most traders, even the most successful ones, trade in obscurity. They make and lose money every minute, hour, day, week, and year. They are successful or they lose on their own merit, using their own faculties. Trading is a very solitary endeavor, and in order to succeed you need a lot of things; one of the most important of those is the ability to be *alone*—and control your emotions.

As a pseudo- "celebrity" trader, my wins and losses are out there in the open a lot of the time. I turned a relatively small amount of money into over $4 *million* back in 1999/2000. I turned roughly $13,000 into over $3.8 million in 2008/2009. These are *headlines*, they are part of my resume, yes, but they are part of any marketing campaign I've done as well, and that's what initially grabs someone's attention, just like "four out of five dentists surveyed recommend Trident gum" is a headline. Wow, four out of five dentists, that's awesome, I'm chewing Trident, baby! Well, in my case, my monetary gains are my calling card. Of course, in between those gains there have been other major gains and some very painful major losses as well. One of the realities of trading is that for every million a good trader makes, he probably lost three or four or even six or seven million to get there. You can't net a million dollars as a full or part time trader without suffering the pain of losing your share to get there. I tell clients all the time that if you can't handle losing, you'll ultimately lose it all. I mean it.

Yet, when most newbies meet me online in our Legends of Wall Street chat room at Affinity Trading, they are stuck on the headlines,

1

the gains. They picture themselves using the stock market as their own personal money tree. I can't tell you how many thousands of people who start mentoring programs with me will say, and it's almost verbatim—"Waxie, I want to be like you, I want to turn my $5,000—or $10,000, or whatever—into millions … that's my goal!"

That's a great goal, right? *Wrong-oooooo!* It's not a great goal, it's a horrible one. It's one that in my experience inevitably will lead to most anyone blowing up their account and turning whatever amount of money they are trading with into *nothing*. Hey, man, as I said I've suffered my share of losses and that includes blowing my own account up on more than one occasion. And, typically, the reason why traders blow themselves to smithereens, whether they are stone-cold newbies, or longtime veteran traders, is because they got caught with their hands in the cookie jar far too often. They took too many "shots." They decided that Wall Street was renamed Vegas Street and that their accounts were actually gambling adjuncts where they closed their eyes and—*let it ride!*

Well, we all know how that ends more than 90 percent of the time—the ride is over and the car don't start no more cause you can't afford any more gas.

Nearly every year since I started teaching traders in 1999, we've done at least one live seminar in Las Vegas, and at each and every one of those seminars I ask the question that I already know the answer to: How many of you have gambled? Almost everyone who comes to a trading seminar in Las Vegas is also going to spend some time in the casino, or playing poker, or betting horses, or doing things that need to stay in Vegas. The follow-up question is another no-brainer: How many of you have *won* gambling? Typically, about 5 percent of my clients say they made money, but I've done seminars where it was more like 2 or 3 percent at best. And, the thing is, that's perfectly fine. Most things in moderation are fine to do, even enjoying yourself gambling knowing you are likely to lose.

And, as the saying goes: What happens in Vegas stays in Vegas … *including your money!*

Setting Goals

What I suggest is that you set *realistic goals*, not pie-in-the-sky get-rich-quick goals. So then, the question is—what is a realistic goal?

There's no magic formula, no one-size-fits-all answer to that. It depends on many variables, but I'll try to break down what I would consider realistic:

Account Value	Daily Goal
$5,000	$100 to $200
$10,000 to $20,000	$200 to $300
$25,000 to $50,000	$300 to $500
$50,000 to $100,000	$500 to $1,000+
$100,000 to $500,000	$1,000 to $5,000
$500,000 to $1 million+	$1,000 to $10,000+

Clearly you can see by this list that there's no quantifiable statistically accurate way to say—*this* is what you should be shooting for! If we get grossly general, I tell clients a realistic goal is 2 percent of whatever your portfolio is, but obviously in this case the larger your portfolio that may or may not hold true. If you have a $10 million portfolio, I would probably say making $200,000 is tough to shoot for. But, you can see by the above list that with many size portfolios that may actually be doable and realistic.

Ultimately, it's really going to depend on a number of factors. Trading is one of those endeavors where everyone has their own "thumbprint" that is unique, even if it's minutely. There's no straight line in trading; it's very much like life itself. There are ebbs and flows, and sometimes there are tsunamis or grand slams, but the one goal that is consistent is to work within yourself and what your comfort level is. If you want to make $500 a day and you have a $10,000 to $25,000 portfolio, that's doable, *but*, and it's a big *but*, you'll likely have to trade options, which we'll talk about later in the book, since there are Securities and Exchange Commission (SEC) day trader restrictions that come into play with any portfolio under $25,000.

1 Percent a Day Keeps the Ka-Chingos Comin'!

Sometimes I tell clients that I want them to shoot for 1 to 2 percent and I get weird looks, as though that's *soooo* little! I'm not a mathematician, but suffice to say if you compound $100 a day every day for a year, which is roughly 200 trading days, and you started with $5,000, that would be well over $25,000, or a 500 percent return on your money in a year. Who wouldn't be happy making 500 percent a year? I certainly would, and anyone who is setting those real-istic goals would be. So, slow and steady is the best way to attain wealth, in spite of it perhaps not being as exciting as you might envision going into trading. Just keep in mind that while the goal in general might be 1 to 2 percent a day, you will have your share of losing days unless you have found some sort of Nirvana of trading. Suffice to say, we'll need to get you prepared to lose in order to have a significant overall *gain!*

Don't Be in Such a Rush to Lose Your Money

Finally, for those of you who are in a rush to make a lot of money, my message couldn't be clearer: It was nice knowing you for the very brief period of time you read this book, because you have a better chance of wrestling a great white shark with blood in the water and surviving than you do getting rich quick as a trader. I've seen it count-less times; I had one client who was a subscriber to my option trader service, and he said he was going to make a million dollars, starting with $20,000. So, he took one of my option ideas and he went all-in, buying $20,000 worth of call options according to his own account. And, because I am pretty good at what I do, if I recall, he doubled his money, making more than $20,000!

Great, right? Yup, it would have been if he then showed restraint and used some of what we cover in the next chapter—money man-agement. Instead, as you probably guessed by now, he let it all ride on my next idea!

And, even though I'm good at what I do and I'd stack my option play ideas against anyone out there, I am wrong sometimes. And, this time I was wrong. So, Mr. All-In went from being up 100 percent to losing all his gains *plus* his original $20,000.

And, that's what is likely to happen to you if you try to get rich quick.

Don't be in such a rush to lose your money! With that, I wish you a *slow* and *steady* trading career.

CHAPTER 2

Bear with Me

Traders and investors are very familiar with *bears*. The market is seen as a constant battle between *bulls* and *bears*. Ironically, in the kingdom of animal spirits, the *bear* represents the forces that ground us. It's strength incarnate. The bear in all of us allows us to have courage, to overcome adversity, and for those of us who face our demons in life, it supports our healing, both physically and—perhaps more important to our life as a trader—emotionally.

One of the first things I do with *any* trader, whether the individual is a total stone-cold newbie or has been trading for over 20 years, is discuss the person's *weaknesses*.

Why's that? Because good traders know why they make money, but what they may not be aware of is why they don't make *more* money. As humans, we often have limited awareness of our Achilles' heels.

Many of us know the story of Achilles. In Greek mythology, when Achilles was a baby, it was foretold that he would die young. To prevent his death, his mother Thetis took Achilles to the River Styx, which was supposed to offer powers of invulnerability, and dipped his body into the water. But as Thetis held Achilles by the heel, his heel was not washed over by the water of the magical river. Achilles grew up to be a man of war who survived many great battles. But one day, a poisonous arrow shot at him was lodged in his heel, killing him shortly after. Hence, the term Achilles' heel!

I myself have experienced this in my trading life, and even in other aspects of my life. I'm really good at finding trends, and mapping out plans, but sometimes I take other trades that don't have the same "hit rate" or quantifiable winning percentage that the trends

5

I've followed and trusted for 15 years do. I will therefore put myself in a position where my best trends are being traded as a "gut" trade, or some less reliable technical pattern. Like many traders, I am ADHD to the max, and patience is not a virtue I have found a lot of time for in my life.

I thus put myself in a position where my best trades work and I *should* make money, but I have given back profits—sometimes partially and sometimes fully—and if I get really silly, I lose and am too frustrated to take a trade that I have a proven track record making money on!

I can't possibly relay to you the vast amount of times I've had clients who, despite me being on a really long roll of winners, will tell me how they lost. Why? Because their Achilles' heel(s) were causing them to fear taking a trade at the right time, or worse, causing them to seek another trade that doesn't have nearly the track record. They guess, hoping to be right, or they enter the trade sorry they missed the correct entry, hoping they can make it up and still cash in. No matter how many times I bang the drum that you shouldn't chase a play, every trader I've ever met will do so at some—or many—points. While they are buying, we're selling them the shares, having reaped a nice profit oftentimes.

The Achilles Have It

There are as many potential Achilles' heels as there are traders! I could spend an entire book writing about all the flaws of traders I've experienced over the last 15 years, but that would bore me and I'm sure you as well. Hell, it might bore you enough to make a foolish trade trying to escape the boredom … and we definitely don't want that!

What I am much more interested in is how we use our bear spiritual guide, which some of us will align with more than others, to help us *heal* our Achilles so when we go into battle no poison darts can kill us. We may get wounded, we may sometimes be on trader life support, but we remain in battle and continue to patch up whatever flaws we have until we are much better traders.

Identifying Your Achilles' Heel

Step 1 is identifying your Achilles' heel(s). If you can't do this, then you are likely to fall prey to it/them over and over again until you are doomed, your account is at zero, and you are best to give up and try something else.

So, first, being honest with yourself is integral to your success, and ultimately in constantly improving your performance. Even the most brilliant, successful traders want to do better if they are interested in improving themselves.

So, how do we identify our flaws?

Ah, let's do it step by step.

Step 1: Identify Your Strengths

This time let's start with your *strengths*. Get a notebook and take 15 minutes (a real 15 minutes) and truly think about what strengths you bring to the table as a trader. If you are a newbie, great, write down the attributes you have that you feel will make you a good, or perhaps, great trader. For example:

Discipline

Patience

Good rule follower

Know the value of money (I had to learn this one the hard way!)

Have your priorities straight

And so on …

Even if you feel it's silly, no one is grading this—it's for *your* edification. No one else will ever see it if you don't want them to. And, if this part is lacking because you aren't aware of your strengths, that's okay as well. Then write down the things you *want* to be strong with as your sort of wish-list, let's call it.

Step 2: Fake It' Til You Make It!

Now let's go through your level of experience, in trading preferably, but also experience in other careers, jobs, or even your love life. What experience do you have that makes you think you can succeed as a trader? Perhaps you are good at making dinner for 25 guests at Thanksgiving and you have the wherewithal to deal with adversity. Perhaps you are an accountant and so you know the value of money, and you have a lot of discipline to follow rules. Whatever you feel gives you the "right" to succeed as a trader, write it down on a separate piece of paper in your notebook.

This will allow you to identify how your strengths have already served you, whether it's as an old-time successful trader or a plumber. I think most people can succeed at trading if they have some of the main attributes we are discussing, or they can learn to train themselves to attain those attributes: Discipline, money management, and overcoming adversity are three of the main ones.

In this step, act as if you are interviewing for a job with me for a trader position. How would you sell me without completely out-and-out lying?

Even if you don't believe any of what you are writing, that's okay. There's a 12-step program that suggests that newcomers "Fake it' til you make it!" sometimes we don't fit into our clothes once we try them on a few times and they are too small for us, but we make some small dietary changes and *voila!* we fit into our new pair of jeans. Don't worry, that's not lying unless you exaggerate your potential to such a degree as you'll never fit into it. So, be realistic, but aim high. No one gets a job for the first time feeling like the perfect fit; typically, you have to grow into it. Allow yourself the possibility that you *can* grow into your potentials—fake it' til you make it!

Step 3: Achilles' Time

Now, it's Achilles' time! Now we need to be brutally honest, keep the built-up potential, but be brave enough—be the *bear*, and dig deep into yourself to pull out all the things you feel will get in your way of being as successful as you like. If you are successful, what's preventing you from being more successful? Take a third piece of paper and take another 15 minutes and delve deep. Not so deep that you tear yourself to shreds telling yourself how horrible you are (that is an Achilles' heel in and of itself, one I've encountered many times with clients over the years).

Many of us are trained to self-criticize so much that we feel guilty for having any positive attributes at times. I am one of those people. I was taught early on in life that my opinion didn't matter, that I would accomplish very little, and that I'd be lucky to get a job as a bank clerk. No offense to those among us who are bank clerks, but typically bank clerks I know (I was one!) want to be promoted at some point; they don't aspire to be a bank clerk forever. I just was rarely, if ever, given positive encouragement. The only time I recall being given such feedback was when I played baseball and pitched. That was the one, and only, thing I recall being confident about ... until I blew my arm out at 15 and was never able to throw the ball again with any real purpose. It blew my mind up, because I had no self-esteem about anything else. I got very depressed when I couldn't do the one thing I loved as a child. So, listen, I get it if you are a low-esteem/low-confidence individual. Unfortunately there are too many of us who were given that message and who were taught to believe it. I'm here to tell you that it's not true; if you're reading this book, then it's likely you have the innate ability to grow, learn, and excel. The belief in that will come in time. For now, I need you to focus on your real Achilles' heels, and one of them just may be your lack of focus, or your negative attitude that nothing will ever work for you.

I've heard clients from around the world at times tell me they can't succeed, they always "take the losers" and it'll "never change."

Yeah, you know what? It won't ... unless we can get you to keep, as I said in Step 2, faking it' til you make it!

Step 4: Analyzing the Data

So, now that we have a good grasp on your strengths, the things you aspire to and what your flaws are, we can analyze that data and figure out a game plan on your best path to success.

Here's how we do that: Take your top three in each step, the three best attributes, the three things you most aspire to, and the three most deadliest of flaws you have. You there? Great, write them all on another separate Step 4 page(s).

Take the three top flaws from Step 3, your top Achilles' heels, and cross out the ones that relate to your Step 1 attributes. Leave the ones that don't apply. You may have none left, or all three; it's okay. There is no right answer. Most of you will have all three left I suspect since these are your top three positives and your top three challenges to overcome. If you do have some crossed out, then my guess is you haven't dug deep enough on your Achilles' heels and I'd start that process again—digging even deeper!

Now take all that's left and cross-check it with the things you aspire to, Step 2. Here you should start to see some scratch-offs—but *don't* scratch these off! Just put check marks next to each of the things you have as flaws that are covered by what you aspire to.

Now, I want you to *add* any of the things you aspire to—use the entire Step 2 list, not just the top three—that you didn't list in Step 3. I suspect many of you will find at least one or two or more traits you aspire to that aren't under your Step 3.

Add those to Step 3. Now you should have a pretty complete idea of all the things we need to work on. You have the top challenges, and you have the lesser ones.

How the Steps Work

STEP 1—Take 15 minutes and WRITE DOWN all your strengths—be as thorough as possible!

STEP 2—Now, pretend you are interviewing for a job and you are trying to sell yourself—WRITE DOWN all the strengths you aspire to have, or others have told you that you have but you aren't as secure in them as you would like.

STEP 3—WRITE DOWN all your WEAKNESSES—your Achilles' heels! ALL OF THEM! Don't be shy; no one else should see this unless you want him or her to!

STEP 4—ANALYZE the data using the blueprint I map out in the Step 4 section. Let's get as accurate a "selfie" as you can of yourself!

Okay, so now here's what I want you to do—the Step 3 items that are *not* on your Step 2 items you aspire to—add them to Step 2.

You need to aspire to them.

You now have a very good idea of what you need to do to improve your trading, whether you are a newbie or a seasoned pro.

CHAPTER

3

Breakout City and Riding the Horse to Gains

The horse spirit guide is representative of speed, adapting to change, grace, and swiftness. There are tons of legends regarding the wisdom of horses, and in fact one of the fastest and newest types of therapy (for humans) is equine therapy. Don't laugh if you've never heard of it, or even if you have, I've done it many times. I found it quite illuminating at times, and what is useful to us as traders is that horses have a unique ability to read the emotions of those around them. They can sense when we are fearful, or nervous, or angry—or calm and at peace.

One of the easiest trends to play really embodies the animal spirit of the horse. It's so simple that anyone with any level of experience, or lack thereof, can take advantage of, have a huge edge and trade it effectively—and profitably!

In the simplest of terms, we call them *breakouts* and *breakdowns*. It's self-explanatory; we search for stocks that are making new highs or new lows. It really is that simple, except we break down these breakouts and breakdowns in several tradable manners.

The 10 a.m. Intraday Break

Oftentimes, the market changes its directional trend intraday. It'll start out one way and then take a turn and reverse. There's what I dub the "10 a.m. rule" that I've tracked for 15 years, and it's a high percentage winner, but—as I'll detail in this chapter, it's not ultimately

11

the best breakout/breakdown trend we have. It is very easy to play and valuable for those of you who either do, or want to trade the market intraday. Basically, we are simply using the time frame of 9:30 and 10 a.m. EST to bracket the high and low during that time frame.

As you can see in Figure 3.1, FB *Gaps up* and then craps out, falling consistently for much of the rest of the day. You could have faded the *gap*, shorting FB at the open, or using our 10 a.m. rule, which I'll detail more upcoming, you can see a really nice entry near 10 a.m., which scored a nice profit to the *short side!*

If we take the high and low from 9:30 to 10:00 a.m. EST, we then use that to guide us on which direction we play the break, or to stand aside because neither range is breached at any point.

Typically, this play is tradable until roughly 2 p.m. EST on any given day.

The Play

At 10 a.m. EST we now have the official bracket, so we take the high and the low of that half hour, and if the stock breaks *below* the *lows* of that time frame/bracket, we can short it. If, on the other hand, it breaks above the *high* of that time frame/bracket, it is a candidate to take *long*.

So, for example, if EBAY opens at 9:30 a.m. at $57.39 and between 9:30 and 10 a.m., it trades with a low price point of $56.92 and a high price point of $57.63, a break below $56.92 after 10 a.m., but before 2 p.m. EST would indicate a trigger to *short* EBAY. So, to be precise, if EBAY trades at $56.91, you'd be short the stock. If, on the other hand, it trades above $57.63, or at $57.64 or above after 10 a.m., but before 2 p.m. EST, then it triggers *long*. The cool thing about this play is that your *stop loss* is defined clearly. You can adjust it according to your risk tolerance and other factors you decide, but the simple stop on EBAY if you end up shorting it would be a break in the *opposite* direction above the 10 a.m. *high!* So, if you enter a *short* on EBAY at $56.91 and it ends up moving against you, your stop is at $57.64.

If you enter a *long* on EBAY on the long price trigger, your stop loss is the opposite; it's defined at $56.91. This is about as simple a trade as we can make intraday. It's a *day trade only!* This is not a trade we hold overnight, and in fact in the Power Trading chapter I'll discuss further how you can manage a trade such as this using

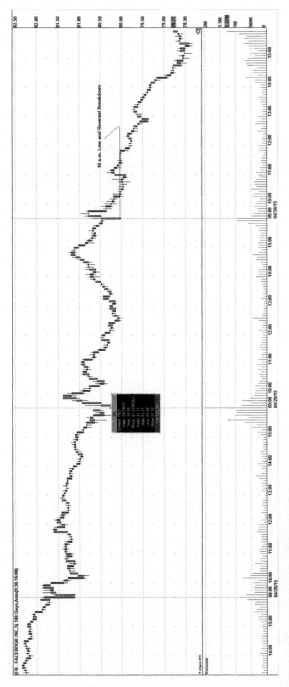

Figure 3.1   Intraday Breakdown 9:30 a.m.

13

time frames, but for now, let's keep it simple and say that you manage it using the parameters above, and let's throw in this factor:

Your *range* for EBAY based on the 10 a.m. rule is $56.92 and $57.63; that's a range of $0.71 between the high and low. That is what you use to trail your stops and that is what you use as your first target to take profits. You want your trades to be at least one-to-one risk/reward ratios. In many non–day trades we try to get two- or three-to-one risk/reward situations, but for intraday we want to try to look at one-to-one to start with. I mean, trying to get $5 out of EBAY intraday in 99.9 percent of all days, at least, is going to be impossible; it just doesn't trade with that kind of velocity. But, $0.71, yes, EBAY can trade out of a breakout pattern for $0.71.

The other factor is, as I stated, time. Typically, this trade is about a one- to two-hour trade, sometimes even less. It really depends on what time you enter. If you enter at 10:01 using a range break, which does happen more often than you'd guess, you will likely want to exit before noon, at least some of the position. And, once you take some of the position off, you'll want to reset your stop to trail by a tighter stop; let's say for this example maybe you move your *stop loss* to $0.50. It sounds arbitrary mainly because it is somewhat so. As you start to see what stocks trade in what ranges and at what velocity and volatility, you'll begin to get a feel for where your stops should be.

You can't possibly use a $0.50 stop on Google (GOOGL). I mean, you can, but it's likely you'll get stopped out the majority of the time. On a stock that is over $500 that trades in a big range (GOOGL often trades in a $5+ range) you'll need your stops to be at least $2 to $3 and maybe even $5 or $6.

You can see a fade in the opposite direction of the Facebook (FB) chart in Figure 3.2 using GOOGL as an example. The fade shown in Figure 3.2 works like a charm, but you'd want to set a realistic stop loss on it—as I stated, anywhere from $2 to $6 is fine by me.

Conversely, a stock like Bank of America (BAC), you'd be silly to use a $0.50 or $0.71 stop; the stock rarely trades with more than a $0.20 to $0.30 cent range, and often it's $0.10 to $0.15 or *less!* So, you're just wasting your time setting that stop on an intraday trade. On a swing trade lasting days, or weeks, or months, and so on that's a different story, but on a pure day trade, you need to know and learn how wide the typical ranges are for the stocks you are looking to trade.

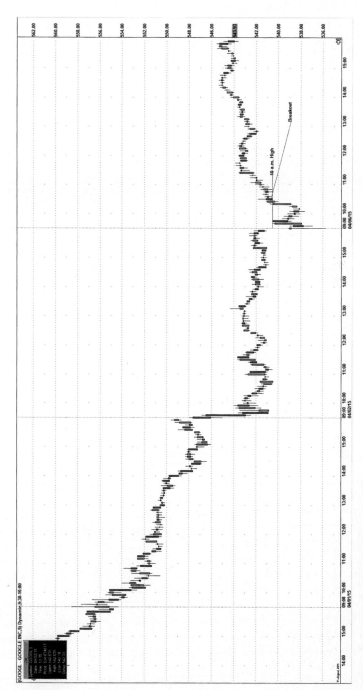

Figure 3.2 Chart of Google (GOOGL)

The Technical Breakout

There are tons of ways to play breakouts via technical analysis. I'm going to just cover a few because I think going over 250 chart patterns with you is a different book. I'm not sure technical analysis, or TA, has many animal spirits, though I suppose it's like the horse in that it can provide stability and calm, because when a pattern sets up right and it's clear as day, it takes a lot of the thinking out of the equation.

Some of the simple patterns with which to trade breakouts and breakdowns off of are shown in Figure 3.3.

Once the stock clears its all-time high at the time over $45 area it just *za-zooms* like it was shot out of a cannon. This is called a *blue skies breakout,* a stock that breaks its all-time high. It's an easy trade setup, and one that has worked extremely well over the years a countless number of times for us!

The 52-Week-High Breakout

One of the simplest and absolutely most-effective trades can be used as both a day trade and/or a swing trade. It's what I call a "thing of beauty" in terms of when it sets up and works because the moves can be so dramatic and so fast that you can make a huge score with very little downside risk if you use proper money management as discussed in Chapter 1.

One of the beautiful things about trading is oftentimes that *simple is best…* and this is mad simple!

We scan through market data you can easily get through a wide variety of places. Yahoo.com Finance is one, but you can Google "52-week highs" or "all-time stock highs" and get a whole bunch of free data for that day's trading, or recent trading.

Trading a stock based on a 52-week high or based on a 52-week low is as simple as that. We are seeking stocks that hit new 52-week lows or highs. If they break out above that 52-week high level, they are an automatic *long*. If they break down below that 52-week low, they are an automatic *short*.

This is a very high percentage play—*very*. I'd guesstimate it works more than 75 to 80 percent of the time, it's that accurate and it gives you potentially that two- or three-to-one risk/reward ratio because the moves can be so powerful, and your stop loss is well defined; you're just using a standard stop loss depending on what the stock's

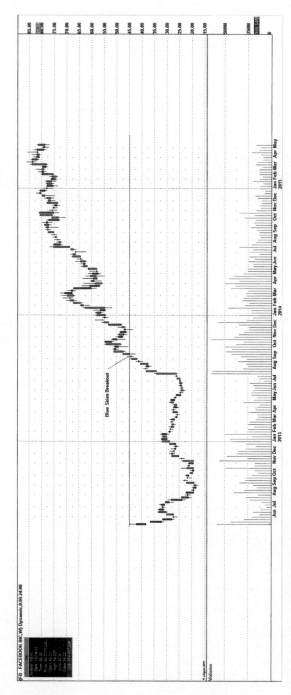

Figure 3.3   FB Blue Skies Breakout

typical daily range is. If it drops below that level and you're long, then you're out. If it rallies above that level and you're short, then you're out.

When we go over options this is one trend you can usually use options (calls or puts) on and make yourself a really nice risk/reward while defining your maximum risk as the price of the option. But, I'll go over that in more detail later. For now, suffice to say trading 52-week high or low breakouts is a very sweet and usually rewarding trade.

Why? Well, even defining that is easy and simple. All you're doing is following the money flow. Money chases stocks up or it runs out of them, leaving them to fall lower. And, those moves usually have follow through when a stock has a clean break out over and under 52-week highs or lows. All we are doing is following the money.

Buy Low and Sell High?

You've heard the expression *buy low and sell high* a gazillion times if you've followed the market, well—ever! It's as old an adage as there is one in terms of the financial markets. But, as a trader we learn that it's even better—often *much* better—to buy high and sell higher, and sell low and cover lower.

There's another old adage you may have heard—*never try to catch a falling knife!* And, another—*never step in front of a freight train!*

Here's one more: A falling knife will still cut your hand open if you try to catch it half an inch from the floor!

And … well, you get my point, we're not in the business of picking when a stock has gone up too much, or down too much. Yes, there are technical patterns we play where it may make sense, but in my experience—not this one. That's more of the power of this trend.

You can see on the chart in Figure 3.4 on Groupon (GRPN) that if you kept trying to find the lows on the stock, you'd probably be reading this book from a nice cardboard house. This is a perfect example of why going *with* the trend is imperative. If you *shorted* every dead-cat bounce on GRPN, you'd have made enough to live in a mansion, or at least earn the right to visit one! Trying to catch falling knives is a very bad idea. Just when you think a stock can't go any lower … it does!

Just like GRPN, you can look at stock charts of stocks like Cliffs Natural Resources (CLF) and Vale SA (VALE) from 2014 and early 2015 and you'll see they followed an eerily similar chart

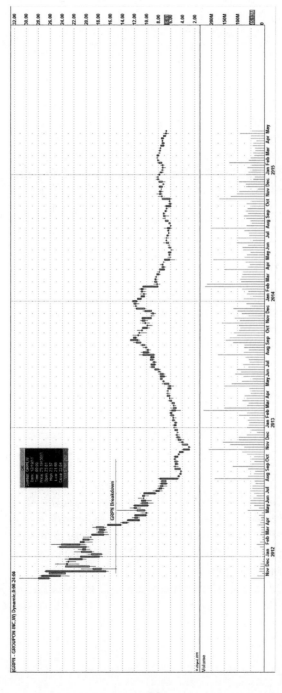

Figure 3.4 GRPN

pattern—every single time the stock bounced it reversed and went lower. That's what's called lower highs and lower lows and is a pattern that we want to track for *short* entries.

Now look at the opposite, look at Apple (AAPL) over the last year or so and you'll see a stock that rampaged higher, making higher highs and *higher* lows. Figure 3.5 is a chart that you want to watch the stock for drawdowns and enter to the long side. Yes, you could be wrong; you could pick the top, just as you could pick the lows on VALE or CLF at some point, but look how many times you would have been right if you bought on every pullback versus how many times you'd be wrong if you did the opposite—obviously.

You can see from the charts in Figures 3.5 to 3.7 that in these examples my point is proven out. Yes, I cherry-picked stocks where I know the trend worked, but I could show you hundreds of examples and the trend works most of the time. Track it for yourself!

Oftentimes, these types of stocks get upgraded or downgraded based on what pundits refer to as *valuation*. AAPL is too high, it's stretched on *valuation!* CLF has hit a point where it's too low and the valuation makes a lot of sense now!

I say phooey on most analysts. Yes, at some point a stock is overvalued or undervalued, sure. The market is a simple equation ultimately—a stock or the overall market goes up because there are more buyers than sellers, and it goes down because there are more sellers than buyers, right?

But, as traders, it's not our job to worry about P/E ratios and whether or not a stock that is down 70 percent on the year and hitting new 52-week lows has finally found a place it can rally up from. I can show you the graveyards of traders filled with those who have traded that way. And, trust me, I've made that mistake myself too many times, so I know firsthand how silly it is to even try to time markets that way—unless there is a trend that counters the move, which there is, and we'll discuss it later on. It's called the January effect, and it happens once a year, and as long as you respect the trend, you won't get caught going against it, anyway. That's what you have me for!

Suffice to say, these breakouts typically provide very strong and very high success rates overall historically and can be a highly effective tool in your trader toolkit!

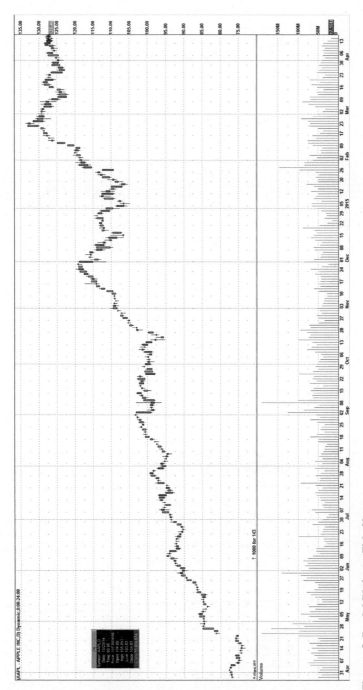

Figure 3.5 AAPL from This Year

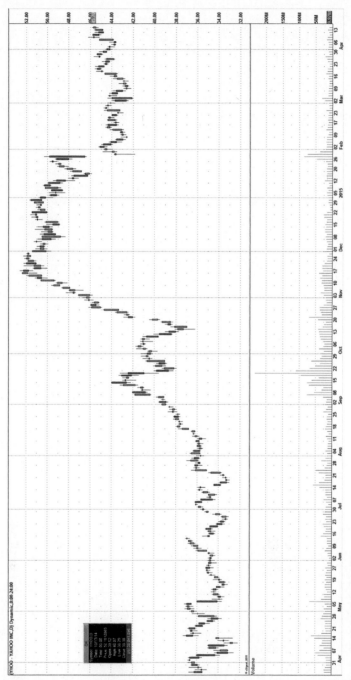

Figure 3.6 YHOO 2015

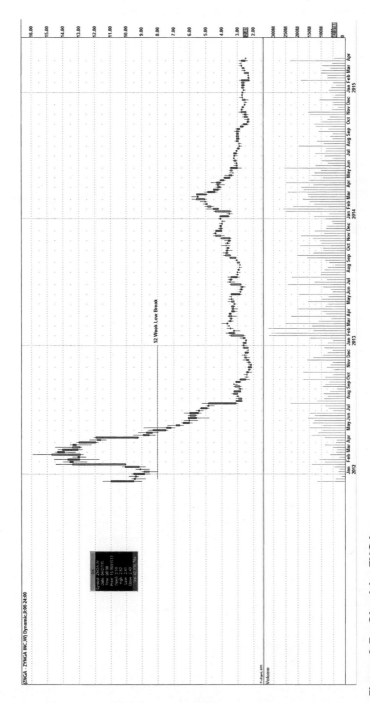

Figure 3.7 Chart for ZNGA

The All-Time-High Blue Skies Breakout

Now, let's look briefly at an even better trend breakout play—the blue skies breakout! Blue skies breakouts are when a stock hits an *all-time high*. It's just called an *all-time low* if it breaks to all-time lows. But, blue skies shows that a stock is being heavily backed and the money flow has sustained enough to push the stock over all possible technical or other resistance. You'll find that many stocks bump against all-time highs and consolidate, not breaking out for a while, and then all of a sudden—*Bammo!* They break out to all-time highs and are off to the proverbial races, with money chasing them even as they scream higher and higher!

Conversely, when stocks break down to all-time lows, it can be a very powerful breakdown and lead to a stock that is in freefall, with no one wanting to try to pick the bottom.

Look at Zynga (ZNGA); it's what I call a *pig dog*. It just continues to make lower and lower lows. Rumor of buyout? Short it! Rumor that it is turning things around? Short it! You just cannot try to pick bottoms! ZNGA makes lows and continues on down. Where does it stop? Can it go lower? I mean, it has to reverse at some point, right? Well, for brief spurts, sure, but why can't it go to $0.25? $1.00? I'm not saying it will, but it certainly can. As traders, we need to look at charts like ZNGA and either short it or stay away!

The horse is a powerful, yet graceful animal, and its spirit is present when we talk about breakouts. Like a good trader, horses are intuitive; they can sense movement and trends. But, it takes time to be intuitive. For some people, it comes very naturally; they have an almost sixth sense about how and why stocks and the markets move. Mostly, they have to learn to trust their gut. The breakout trends here are a way to "cheat" intuition, because the market is doing all the work for you. All you have to do is follow the money and the market will do the rest.

CHAPTER 4

Power Trading

If you're lucky, the panther is your spirit animal!

The Panther: The panther symbolizes courage, valor, and power. If the panther is your power animal, you are blessed with a fierce guardian. The panther totem animal encourages us to understand the power within the shadows and to acknowledge these powers to help eliminate our fear of the dark and unknown.

When we relate that to trading and the type of trader you are, we talk about being a full-time trader and using all the powerful tools that we can gain mastery over. Many traders fall prey to their own fears, or self-doubts; the trader who is a panther may have those same fears and doubts, but makes the choice to move forward despite them. They choose to power trade!

So, what is power trading?

For me, power trading is all-day trading. It involves using and learning several techniques, some in this book and some perhaps derived from other sources. As I always state to clients, I'm not the only game in town—there are other great traders who have techniques that work for them and may work for you, too. Wisdom is derived from various sources. Although I am hoping that I become one of your main teachers, you'd be wise to seek council from other valuable sources as well.

What works for me may not work for you. The techniques and the actual stock ideas aren't really the issue; the issue is searching for and finding those that work for you. You are unique, your style is unique to you, your issues are unique to you, and your portfolio is unique to you. You are you.

While your challenges, issues, and the amount of money you are trading with isn't going to be completely unique to you—as a whole *you* definitely are unique! Embrace that, don't run from it and hide thinking you are somehow "wrong" to be you. Too many people fall into that rut where they think they should be someone else and somehow that would make their lives better. Would I like to be Brad Pitt for a while? Sounds nice, but I'm quite sure that Mr. Pitt has his own challenges. I mean maybe Angelina Jolie is really hard to be in a relationship with. Or, Lord knows, they have a ton of kids; that can't possibly be easy to handle! Regardless, it doesn't even matter since I don't have the choice to be anyone but … *me!*

And, you don't have the choice to be anyone but … *you!* And, like the panther, we need to embrace the courage that makes us ourselves and find what works for us. Who our teachers are a good place to start.

Now, if you decide power trading is for you, or you may grow into power trading, then this chapter is going to be helpful to you!

Be You … Be Powerful!

I think of a power trader as someone who is capable of trading the market successfully throughout the entire day, and when desired, before and after regular market hours as well. If you already have trading experience, then you know that many diverse opportunities come and go each day in the market, and that trading them successfully requires a broad range of skills. To trade successfully throughout the day, you need to use a variety of tools, techniques, and strategies. You also need to adapt quickly to changing market conditions. Trading a.m. gaps, p.m. laggards, breaking news events, or trading after-hours requires different strategies. Power traders have the experience, agility, and skills needed to recognize and take advantage of the various trading opportunities that come and go each day in the market. Although it's not necessary to trade on a full-time basis or all day every day to be a power trader, power traders have the expertise to do so when they so choose. It's all about choice. Once *you* decide you are a *panther* and you want to *power trade*—now you must learn and develop the skills necessary to become a *power trader!*

Intraday Primer

It may seem simple on some level. To be an all-day trader—a power trader—I merely need to press buttons all day and trade. Hence,

I'm a panther ready to pounce, bro! I'm powerful! Eh, not so fast, yeah, you can press buttons, hell, any baby can press some buttons, and they can even do it all day, but can they do it and make money consistently? Can they do it and earn a living? That is ultimately what will separate the proverbial "men" and "women" from the "boys" and "girls."

With that said, let's get going. For those of you who might be new to the term, *intraday* is associated with the period of time between the open and close of the market's daily session, though a more liberal interpretation might also include trading before the market opens or after it closes. On a given day in the market, you'll encounter fluctuations in volume, trend continuations and reversals, changes in volatility, and more. Sometimes external events such as world news announcements, industry news releases, or even individual company news releases trigger intraday market swings. Rumors, general market perceptions, perceptions about the state of the economy, or simply the normal ebb and flow of supply and demand also cause intraday moves in the market. Regardless of the cause, a power trader needs to adapt to these changing market conditions. A brief overview of the types of details that a trader may need to manage during a typical day follows. As I just noted, market conditions vary throughout the trading day, particularly those days when it seems at any given moment the news flow can move us plus or minus 100 or more points in a matter of seconds. Part of that is because we live in a world that is now constantly in flux, but then again you could probably say that about most anytime in history. So, what it really is, when you break it down to bare bones, is that the news flow itself just gets to us faster than ever before. Before the advent of the Internet, we got all our breaking news from TV and radio, or even newspapers. Most people had to wait until 6 p.m. or 11 p.m. news shows to get the day's breaking news. CNN made news more readily available, but even that wasn't as fast as Twitter or Google—it wasn't as fast as someone literally at the scene of an event posting news as it happens. News doesn't *break* now, it's in real time! Thus, during the day, and depending on the time of day, different trading strategies apply.

Though many events such as unexpected news releases can move the market in unpredictable ways, there are also daily market rhythms that are predictable to some degree. Traders that become familiar with the market's daily rhythms can develop trading strategies to take advantage of them or to avoid their pitfalls. The intraday time frames chapter breaks down the trading day into a chronological sequence of separate time frames, or time periods, and correlates them to market behavior. You'll find some useful trading tips there as well. Intraday overview preparation for the trading day generally begins with a check of the futures, latest news, and overall market conditions. Next, open positions such as swing trades are reviewed, and throughout the process, traders are always on the lookout for specific stocks to trade.

Power trading stocks that are gapping up or down from their prior day's closing price often provide great trading opportunities, but ideas may come from a variety of sources, including online news services or business news channels such as CNBC. In fact, I think CNBC is a crucial component of any trader's toolkit.

As the trading day gets underway, traders watch for trade setups. The first few minutes after the market opens tend to be very volatile and active. Since this often results in exaggerated price moves, it can be a very profitable time for an agile trader. At this time, stocks that have gapped up or down are often turned over for a quick profit should they make a corrective price reversal. The specifics on how to trade gaps are covered later in the book. As the day progresses and market conditions change, trading strategies are adjusted accordingly. Stop-loss orders may be tightened, positions may be exited, or new positions may be entered into. Laggards, stocks that are lagging behind the market or are lagging behind their peers, often provide new trading opportunities. Throughout the day when appropriate, and as the end of the market's regular session approaches, traders plan exit strategies for their intraday trades. In most cases, traders exit all of their intraday positions by the close of normal market hours each day. Of course, swing trades are also managed throughout the day and beyond according to the original plan for each trade, and depending on overall market conditions. After the market closes, many traders quit for the day. Others continue to watch for after-hours trading opportunities, at which time, breaking news tends to become the dominant factor that influences stock prices and provides trading opportunities.

Before continuing, though, I'll provide a few brief words of caution for those of you who may not have any experience trading outside of regular market hours. Due to lower volume, greater price spreads, and other factors, more risk is associated with after-hours trading. Consequently, you should be more cautious and use limit orders only when trading outside of regular market hours.

Time Frames

Power trading is nothing if it's not about trading time frames. Over 15 years I've tracked market movements and found that consistently certain times of the day the market has certain tendencies. It's important for us to get a general overview of what those *trend*encies are.

In my opinion, one of the most important things about power trading is learning to trade these intraday time frames. At certain times of the day the market trends to be active and volatile. At other times, there may be a lull, or slowdown, in the market's activity. While this behavior is not 100 percent certain to occur exactly the same each day, it does tend to occur with a reasonable degree of regularity. Here is a chronological breakdown of the trading day based on observations I've made over the years.

All times are in Eastern Standard Time (EST):

08:00 a.m.–09:30 a.m. Pre-market (after hours) trading

09:30 a.m.–10:00 a.m. Gap trades

10:00 a.m.–1:00 p.m. 10:00 a.m. rule in effect

1:00 p.m.–2:30 p.m. Lunchtime lull/reversal

2:30 p.m.–3:20 p.m. Post-lunch activity

3:20 p.m.–3:40 p.m. Afternoon lull

3:40 p.m.–4:00 p.m. Market on close/EOD

4:00 p.m.+ After-hours, news rules!

Referring to the preceding time frames, it's easy to see why you need to adjust your trading strategies throughout the trading day. For example, trading gaps obviously requires different techniques than trading the lunchtime lull, and trading the lunchtime lull is different than trading after-hours.

Figure 4.1 is a daily chart that shows how the Nasdaq composite behaved during the various time frames that are discussed.

As you can see on this particular day the market acted much as I describe in this chapter. Again, hindsight is 20/20 if it were an isolated incident, but these patterns, in my experience, *trend* to repeat themselves over and over again!

9:30–10:00 a.m.: Gaps

As you can see on the chart in Figure 4.1, the market is usually very active and volatile during the first 30–75 minutes of trading, which is great for traders. High volume and volatility often provide the best trading opportunities. In fact, if the morning goes well, after the first hour or so of trading, some traders may even meet their profit targets for the day and take the rest of the day off. The first 30 minutes of trading is primetime for gaps, especially if the entire market is gapping large. Before the market opens, I look for stocks that are gapping up or down. If I find momentum stocks that are gapping significantly and otherwise look okay to trade, I start watching for a trade entry. Large gaps often result from traders overreacting to news during after-hours (or pre-market) trading when volume is low. When the volume is low, any significant buying or selling pressure after-hours can move a stock's price more dramatically, resulting in exaggerated price moves. Then when the market opens and volume returns to normal, there is frequently a corrective price reversal or price snapback (see Figure 4.1). When trading gaps, the snapback reversal is what I'm looking to trade. To further illustrate this concept, try pulling a rubber band further and further apart. Just when you can't pull it any further without it breaking, let it go. What happened? If it's truly rubber, it will "snap back," and even better, it will often go much further in the opposite direction!

This is what fading a gap equates to, the snapback of a rubber band. If a stock gaps up significantly, I sometimes enter a short position anticipating a corrective pullback to the downside. Conversely, if a stock gaps down, I often enter a long position anticipating a corrective snapback to the upside, as occurred on the chart. Trading gap snapbacks in either direction is called fading the gap. Of course, like everything else about the market, it does not behave exactly the same on any given day. Though gaps are high percentage plays, particularly in the case of large gap *downs*, there are times when a stock gaps large and keeps on going the same direction without the usual snapback reversal. You will also want to watch and manage your swing trades at this time. If you are holding a swing trade long and it gaps up large, you might want to consider taking advantage of the opportunity to take profits. The same is true if you are short and there is a large gap to the downside. Of course, you need to consider your overall plan for each trade, but if you have sufficient gains,

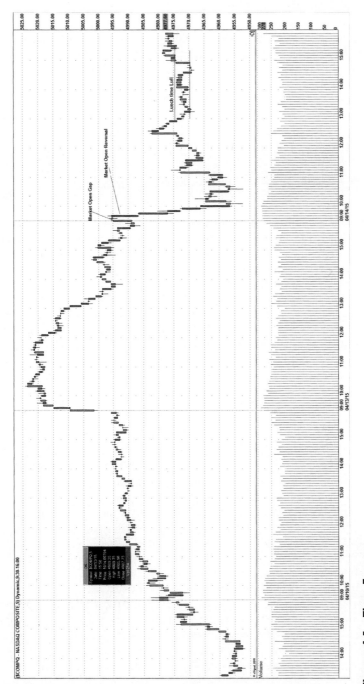

Figure 4.1 Time Frames

a gap could provide a nice opportunity to take profits. Alternatively, if you want to remain in a position, you could consider taking profits and reenter the position at a better price should there be a snapback reversal of the gap. Although, since there is no guarantee that a corrective reversal will take place, you should take that possibility into account before exiting your position. Examples and more detailed information about trading gaps are provided in Chapters 8 and 10. I spend a lot of time on gaps because I think it's one of the simplest plays that anyone can learn, and it offers one of the highest win percentages of any trend I've ever followed. A *gap down* is by far and away my single favorite intraday/power trading trend.

10:00–1:00 p.m.: 10 a.m. Rule in Effect

As discussed in the previous section, prices frequently snap back contrary to the direction of a gap. If you went long on a gap up and the price made a corrective pullback, you would likely take a loss on the trade. The same is true if you shorted a gap down and it made a corrective upside reversal. I created the 10:00 a.m. rule to help avoid getting caught on the wrong side of a trade when trading gaps. The 10:00 a.m. rule is a simple guideline that can help you avoid losing money, and may help you make money, particularly if you are new to trading. Here is the 10:00 a.m. rule: *If a stock gaps up, you should not buy it long unless it makes a new high after 10:00 a.m. Conversely, if a stock gaps down, you should not sell it short unless it makes a new low after 10:00 a.m.* You may need to trade contrary to what your emotions are telling you to do in order to follow this rule because when the market or stocks are gapping up, there may be tremendous enthusiasm on the buy side. People frequently get caught up in the excitement and continue to jump in and buy the gap, or they may simply buy because they don't want to miss out on a potential rally. Alternatively, if it's a gap down, people may panic and sell initially. Following the 10:00 a.m. rule can help keep your emotions in check and prevent a loss if a gap reversal occurs. Though a stock or the market may gap and keep on going, in most cases, there is at least a temporary snapback correction. If gaps are going to reverse, the reversal usually occurs before 10:00 a.m. Eventually, a dominant direction begins to emerge, which may only be temporary, or it could form a trend for the day. Regardless, after the initial gap trading is over, you can also use the 10:00 a.m. rule as a guideline to time potential entries for other trades. If a stock makes a new high after 10:00 a.m., it's a sign of strength. When this occurs, more often than not, an upside trend will continue. Therefore, I frequently enter a long position for a trade when a momentum stock makes a new high after 10:00 a.m. After establishing a position, you should immediately place a stop-loss order to limit your risk, then trail the price up if the trend continues, which it will often do throughout the morning, and possibly beyond on a strong uptrending day. In the case of new lows, you would take the opposite approach. If a stock makes a new low after 10:00 a.m., it's a sign of weakness, so you could enter a short position and limit your risk by using a trailing stop-loss order.

1:00–2:30 p.m.: Lunchtime Lull/Reversal

Some traders believe that lunch begins at 12:00 p.m.; however, the observations I've made while tracking the market's behavior over the years lead me to conclude that the majority of traders break-away for lunch from 1:00 to 2:30 p.m. During the lunch time frame you'll frequently see a slowdown, or lull, in market activity. Volume tends to taper off or dry up as traders take time off for lunch. As a result, the market and individual stock prices will often drift or move counter to the prior trend. It's also not uncommon for the market to reverse directions either during lunch or soon afterward. As always where market behavior is concerned, there are times when pullbacks don't occur, or new highs or lows are made over lunch, but I've observed this behavior for a number of years, and a lunchtime lull occurs a large percentage of the time. For that reason, as the lunch time frame approaches, I either exit my intraday positions, particularly when I have nice gains from riding a morning trade, or I tighten my stop-loss orders.

Even though there are times when a trend continues right on through lunch and beyond, to me, it's just not worth taking the risk. I've experienced too many instances where gains slowly wither away while the market drifts aimlessly up and down through lunch. There frequently just isn't sufficient volume and momentum to sustain prices, and I don't want to risk giving back the morning's gains. However, if on a given day the market appears sufficiently strong, or weak if you are trading short, you could tighten your stop-loss orders as a safeguard rather than exiting your positions. You could also consider reducing your lot sizes by one-half to reduce your risk exposure. At the very least, you should watch your trades closely during the lunch time frame. On the other hand, if you are looking to enter a position, the lunchtime lull often provides a great opportunity to do so. It may also provide a great opportunity to enter a countertrend position. For example, if the market has been trading sideways or slowly trending down into the lunch time frame, an impression may emerge that the market appears to have underlying strength and isn't likely to go much lower. As traders come back from lunch, they might think, "What the heck?" and take a long position. Since volume is low at lunch, it doesn't take a lot of buying to start pushing up prices. As momentum picks up and buying continues, it often results in a strong countertrend reversal. These types of days provide great opportunities for entering countertrend positions during the lunch period.

2:30–3:20 p.m.: Post-Lunch Activity

As traders come back from lunch, market activity generally begins to pick up. Initially, it may not be clear which direction the market will take, but as described in the prior section, it's not uncommon for the market to reverse directions during lunch or shortly afterward. This is the time frame during which the market decides whether it's going to continue a lunchtime reversal or resume the prelunch trend.

3:20–3:40 p.m.: Afternoon Lull

Later in the day, many traders begin taking profits and exiting intraday positions, while others may simply continue riding positions they opened during or after lunch. Some traders may have already quit for the day by this time. In general, it's a time when the market tries to determine where it's going for the rest of the day. It may try to bounce or sell off during this time period as traders juggle their positions. Regardless of the reasons, around the 3:20–3:40 p.m. time frame, I've observed that an afternoon lull in market activity tends to occur with a high degree of regularity. Similar to the lunchtime lull, this afternoon lull provides another opportunity to enter a position for a trade. For example, if you feel the day is going to close strong and there is a pullback during the afternoon lull, you can take advantage of the pullback to enter one or more long positions.

3:40–4:00 p.m.: Market on Close/End of Day

This is the time frame when the market decides how it's going to close. Many institutions need to square away their positions by the end of the day. Any imbalances need to be balanced—hence market-on-close orders can provide some indication of what the market may do. For example, if I'm watching the news wires or listening to CNBC and hear around 3:30–3:40 p.m. that there is strong institutional market-on-close buying due at the close, I'll likely be a buyer for a quick end-of-day trade since it often becomes a self-fulfilling prophecy. Meaning, when traders get the news of market-on-close buying, they perceive the market is going higher so they start buying, which causes the market to go higher, even before the close. It's similar to what happens with key moving average (MA) support levels, particularly the 200-day MA (but others as well). Since the 200-day MA is perceived as a strong level of support, when a price falls to the 200-day MA traders often start buying, which once again creates a self-fulfilling prophecy by reinforcing the notion that the 200-day MA is a strong level of support. Just because this time frame is near the end of the day doesn't mean that I'm buying to hold overnight. If I do enter a position during this time frame, such as a market-on-close *trade* as described above, it's typically for a quick 10–20 minute intraday trade only. While I may hold a market-on-close trade right up to the end of the day (or until the real market-on-close trades come in), in most cases, I will exit the trade before the market closes. Of course, as with all trades, there's no guarantee a given stock will go up, so you still want to employ reasonable risk management strategies and set stop-loss orders accordingly.

8:00–9:30 a.m./4:00–8:00 p.m.: After-Hours, News Rules!

Even though this section applies primarily to trading after the market closes its regular trading session, I'm using the term *after-hours* to refer to trading outside of the market's regular hours of operation, whether it is after the market closes for the day or before the market opens in the morning. Though investors may occasionally buy or sell stocks during after-hours trading, their decisions are likely based on a long-term plan, whereas traders who trade after-hours are generally looking for a short-term trade that can be flipped for a profit during the current after-hours session, or at the longest, a potential gap the next morning. For a long-term investor, after-hours price action may be less of a concern, but for a trader, some event must cause a substantial price swing in a relatively short time period, otherwise, there wouldn't be many, if any, after-hours trading opportunities. Fortunately for after-hours traders, there are events that cause the desired price swings. The main force that propels after-hours price moves is breaking news. Examples include upgrades and downgrades, large company deals, stocks being added to a large index such as the S&P 500, earnings warnings, earnings reports, major world news events, and others. Some news releases drive a stock, sector, or even the entire market up or down. For example, if a large company like INTEL(INTC) comes out with an earnings report that substantially beats estimates, not only is INTC likely to go up, it could take the futures and the entire technology market with it, particularly the stocks that are in the same sector as INTC.

Here is another example. Suppose CISCO (CSCO) releases news that they've reached an inflection point, and orders are starting to pick up significantly. Since CSCO is a widely followed stock that could potentially influence the market, I would immediately start watching CSCO to see if the price takes off. More often than not, there isn't time to catch a ride on the specific stock for which the news was released, or CSCO in this case. If the price does take off, I would look for an opportunity to play other stocks in the same sector such as JNPR and so on. Mainly, I would just start watching competing companies. In the case of big news releases that could potentially move the market overall, I would also look at other popular momentum stocks like EBAY, Amazon (AMZN), Broadcom (BRCM), Apple (AAPL), and so on. Basically, I would take a look at any large momentum stock that is likely to go up with an upside market move and as a result, could potentially be traded after-hours for a quick gain of $0.50 to $1.00 or more. If you set up your after-hours watch list with momentum stocks grouped by sectors, you can quickly check out competing companies when news breaks about a company, whether it impacts the entire market, a specific sector, or other companies in the same industry. For example, I group semiconductor companies such as Intel (INTC), Applied Materials (AMAT), KLA-Tencor (KLAC), and so on together. Similarly, I do the same type of grouping for other sectors, such as Facebook (FB), Twitter (TWTR), and LinkedIn (LNKD). Generally, I'm not looking to hold a position overnight. However, if the news is particularly good and I think the market may gap up the next morning, I may hold one-half of my position until the next morning. But if I do hold any shares, I will generally only do so when I am up on a trade and can close out half of my position with a profit to help offset a potential loss the next morning on my remaining shares. In most cases, though, I prefer to simply take my profits. I would much rather take a $1 to $2 profit, even if it means leaving money on the table, than take the risk of turning a winning trade into a losing trade. Additionally, if you are going to hold a position overnight based on news, you should make sure that you clearly understand the news and read it thoroughly. It's not uncommon for a company to release good news first to soften the impact of other bad news. For example, a company could announce that it beat the street and follow up 15 minutes later with an announcement that the CEO is retiring. A $1 to $2 profit could evaporate in an instant during after-hours trading and turn into a $4 loss, especially considering prices can move quickly during after-hours trading due to relatively low volume and/or large price spreads. As previously mentioned, if you are new to after-hours trading, I recommend that you proceed cautiously at first because there is more risk associated with it. Low volume and/or larger price spreads, among other factors, can make it more difficult to get in and out of positions at a favorable price.

Time Frame Examples

Figure 4.2 shows the price action of Expedia (EXPE) during various intraday time frames. The price action was volatile on this particular day, which provided great trading opportunities. During the first 30 minutes, EXPE opened strong then pulled back. A nice trade would have been to fade the open with a short position. After 10:00 a.m., the price broke through its prior low, which provided another opportunity to enter a short position. Depending on how you executed the trade, you could have taken profits as EXPE made another new low. Otherwise, you would have likely stopped out if you were using a trailing stop and held the position longer. Notice over the lunch time frame, EXPE made a countertrend price reversal. If you had entered a long position in anticipation of a potential lunchtime reversal, you could have gotten out with some nice gains before the next pullback. However, the countertrend move wasn't sustained in this case and the stock eventually closed the day near its lows. Of course, this example applies to a single day only. In many instances,

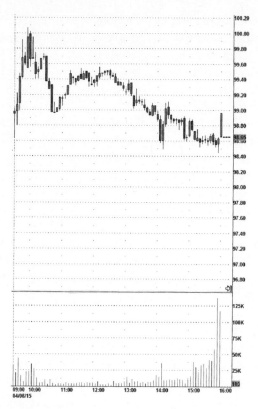

Figure 4.2   Chart for EXPE

a lunchtime reversal continues throughout the rest of the day. Here is another example that shows an intraday chart for the Dow Jones Industrials. Notice in this case that the market gapped up by a small amount and kept going higher. After a brief pause around 10:00 a.m., the uptrend continued into the lunch time frame. You could have potentially traded the trending day by using the 10:00 a.m. rule as a guideline, as described in Chapter 10. Although there was a small pullback during the afternoon lull, a general uptrend continued throughout the day and beyond.

News Trader

News events traders generally follow the news closely. At least I do, and I recommend that you do as well. As I stated, CNBC is a must for me as a trader. Not only does the news provide trading ideas, it may also help prevent losses should breaking news have a negative impact on the market or stocks you are trading. Typically, traders start the day by taking the market's pulse to determine whether there is an upside or downside market bias. The idea is to get a sense of whether anything has already begun to affect the temperament of the market, and if so, to determine what and why. I begin by checking the S&P and Nasdaq futures to get a general sense of the overall market bias. If the futures are up, then the market at large will likely open higher as well. If the futures are essentially unchanged or they are down, the market will likely open flat or lower. Once the overall market bias has been determined, it's time to check the online news wires and TV business news on CNBC or other business channels (you can also check the futures on CNBC). Generally, I just like to catch up on the news because it could influence my trading day, but I also want to see if there are any particular reasons for the market's bias.

A variety of events could potentially influence the market and/or stock prices. Examples include breaking world news events, major company news releases, analyst upgrades or downgrades, earnings announcements, the release of economic data, and so on. Right now, as I write this book, it would be Russia/Ukraine news, the price of oil, the Middle East, and ISIS terrorists. The news flow changes, so by the time you are reading this it may very well be other events, or at least other events in conjunction with the ones we are dealing with right now. However, in some cases there may not be any apparent reason for a bias. A bias could simply be the result of ordinary market fluctuations, trend continuations, or temporary imbalances between the overall supply and demand for stocks.

I also check to see if any particular stocks are being talked about in the news, or if any are moving in pre-market action—major news about a large company could also influence the market. Maybe FB had a good or bad news announcement, or AAPL was downgraded. Whatever the reason, the idea is to determine why the market or certain stocks are up or down since it will influence the trading day, and could provide trading opportunities or affect the performance of positions I currently hold. It's important to continue watching the news wires and CNBC throughout the trading day. Not only do you want to manage your power trades if a major news announcement breaks, the news is a great ongoing resource for trading ideas. More detailed information and examples of how news announcements can influence the market and individual stocks are provided in Chapter 11.

Swing Trades

A stock that is held over a period of multiple days, but not as a long-term investment, is referred to as a swing trade. To minimize risk, I often close out all of my trading positions at the end of each day. However, when a good reason justifies it, I do hold a stock or option position over a longer period of time. On days when I am holding one or more swing trades, after getting a general sense of the overall market, I take any appropriate actions to manage my swing trades based on my original plan for a trade, and whether current market conditions, breaking news, or a desire to take profits justifies a modification of my original plan. I generally remove all of my stop-loss orders before the close of trading each day. Why? Simple, because a breaking-news event could cause a temporary exaggerated price swing, or a gap; I don't want to be arbitrarily stopped out of a position.

For example, if I owned FireEye (FEYE), which is a cybersecurity company, with a stop-loss order placed $1 under its closing price, which as of now is around $42 a share, and FEYE gapped down $2 the next morning, my stop-loss order would trigger but the order would fill $2 less than the prior close, or $1 less than my intended stop-loss limit for managing risk. I'd get filled based on the opening "tick" for the stock, even if it then bounced $3 or just to break even. Stop-loss orders should be lifted before the close of trading each day to avoid such possibilities. Remember that the first tick is often the low or high for the stock on any particular day. Instead, I prefer to manage my trade and control how I exit a position so I can take into consideration overall market conditions, news announcements, or other factors that might influence my stock's price. Although I might not be happy about FEYE gapping down $2, if I'm in control, I have the option of holding out for a potential corrective snapback bounce where I might be able to exit the position at a better price. Or, depending on the price action and market, I might still exit the position with a $2 loss, but at least I would have the option to choose rather than leaving it to a market maker to set the price at which my order fills. Additionally, some market makers may try to intentionally trigger stop-loss orders by temporarily posting and retracting erroneous prices, particularly during after-hours trading where though you can't place a stop loss, you could place a limit order on many platforms and it's easy to "pick you off" for a brief moment, only to reverse the stock and cause you flesh eating zombie pangs in the process. Since I begin each day fresh without stop-loss orders, one of the first things I do is either reset my stop-loss orders or exit positions, depending on the strength of the market and my original plan for each trade. Alternatively, if I'm looking to enter into a swing trade, I evaluate the potential for that as well and plan accordingly.

Gap Me, Baby

I spend a lot of time discussing *gaps,* and probably even repeat myself ... repeat myself, because they are a cornerstone of my trading style and simple enough for even the stone-cold newbie to learn and play!

Great trading opportunities are presented when the market or individual stocks gap up (open higher than where they closed the day before) or gap down (open lower than where they closed the day before) significantly from their prior day's closing price. Therefore, before the market opens I start looking for stocks that are gapping up or down. I look for momentum stocks since they tend to gap more dramatically and provide the best opportunity for a corrective price reversal in the opposite direction. Though not always, momentum stocks often consist of technology or biotechnology (biotech) stocks. Most trade on the Nasdaq stock exchange, and therefore, like most stocks on that exchange they have four letters in their symbols such as AAPL, GOOG, Regeneron Pharmaceuticals (REGN), and so on. Momentum stocks provide greater liquidity and price action, which makes it easier to get in and out of a trade fast, and hopefully, with a nice profit. Once I've picked some good trading candidates, I add them to my watch list and start looking for potential trade setups. Then, it's just a matter of watching the price action and executing a trade, if the setup develops according to my plan for the trade. Gaps offer so many potential trading opportunities that I've devoted a lot more time, and Chapter 10, solely to gap trading. More detailed information and gap examples are provided there.

Laggards

Frequently, the prices of closely related stocks in the same sector or a similar industry move in sync with one another. This means, if the price of one goes up or down, the prices of other similar stocks may follow along. Since the stocks are in a similar business, when an earnings announcement or other news event affects the performance of one, the other stocks are often impacted as well. If you watch these stocks, you may occasionally encounter an intraday price divergence where the prices of some stocks are making a significant move that leaves one or more of the others behind. The comparison could be between as few as two stocks, or it could be a larger group of similar stocks. Any stocks among the group that lag behind the price movement of the others are referred to as laggards. A price divergence between a laggard and its peers will frequently correct itself at some point, either intraday, or sometimes during the following day or so. Depending on overall market conditions, and subject to stock specific news, often the laggard will take off and play catchup. However, the peer stocks could also be the ones that move back toward the direction of a laggard's price. You can use the strength and direction of the overall market as an additional indicator as to which is most likely to make a corrective move. For example, if the market is moving higher and a laggard's peer stocks are moving higher, the laggard is more likely to make a corrective catchup move at some point. Laggards can provide nice intraday trading opportunities.

Market Close

In most cases, traders exit their intraday trades before the regular market session closes. Therefore, during the latter part of the trading day, traders begin watching for exit opportunities. Gains may be locked in with stop-loss orders or trailing stops, or positions are simply exited whenever an appropriate opportunity comes along. At the same time, new trading opportunities may also appear near the end of the day.

After Hours

In today's market, most online brokerage firms, and all direct-access brokers, let you trade outside of regular market hours. You can generally trade both after the market closes, and before the market opens. For purposes of discussion, I'm referring to both as after-hours trading. Since the type of support for after-hours trading can vary between brokers and changes frequently, you should check with your broker for specific information and the hours of operation. Although many traders quit for the day when the market closes, many also continue to watch for after-hours trading opportunities. For the most part, breaking news tends to be the driving force of price action during after-hours trading. Although I occasionally trade after-hours (and once did virtually every day), I don't do it as often now. When I do trade after-hours, I generally trade for about 30 minutes or so after the market closes, though it is possible to trade much later. After-hours trading opens at 4:00 p.m. EST every day, and closes at 8 p.m. EST. Conceivably you could trade for 12 straight hours. I don't think I'd call that power trading, though, more like *insane trading*. Since after-hours trading is primarily news driven, and the bulk of companies release their news shortly after the market closes, a larger percentage of the trading opportunities take place soon after the market closes. Still, late breaking news does present opportunities at later times. If you are new to after-hours trading, proceed cautiously at first because there is more risk associated with after-hours trading. Lower volume and/or larger price spreads, among other factors, can make it more difficult to get in and out of positions at a favorable price, particularly with thinly traded stocks.

CHAPTER 5

$12,500 to $3.8 Million

First off, let's get this out of the way—here is an actual review by an independent accountant to prove that I did indeed do this. It wasn't the first time I did something like it, and hopefully it won't be the last time, but it's obviously significant.

I get asked how I did it all the time, and I rarely engage clients because I don't want *you* to think of the market in these terms. I didn't have a goal to make $3.8 million; frankly, I didn't have *any* goal when I started trading that money. I just had some money in an account, and that was what was in there so that's what I used. There's no magic to that. I didn't say to myself, "Gcc, I have $12,500, I'll start trading today and about 14 months later I'll have $3.8 million!"

I wish it were that simple; I'd do it every 14 months and be swimmingly filthy rich! It's not simple at all; it involved a ton of hard work, a bit of luck, and a lot of inspiration and intuition. It also involved something that is totally out of my control—the market!

Bull, Bear—I Don't Care!

I say this all the time—in fact, I coined this term and others have stolen my catch phrase. That's okay—plagiarism is the highest form of flattery! The fact is, we don't typically care if the market is going up, or down. As long as we are on the right side of the market/trade, that's all that matters ...

Hence: Bull, bear—I don't care!

In 2008, we went into a market tailspin that is almost unparalleled other than the Great Depression. The market sold off dramatically,

CERTIFIED PUBLIC ACCOUNTANTS
420 LEXINGTON AVENUE
SUITE 2450
NEW YORK, NY 10170
PHONE: (212) 972-6490
FAX: (212) 687-2705

**Independent Accountant's Report on Applying
Agreed Upon Procedures**

**Michael Parness
20 River Terrace #8M
New York, NY 10282**

Sir:

At your request we have performed the procedures enumerated below, which were agreed upon by you. These procedures, which were performed solely to assist in the reporting of your trading activities gains/losses, from the information supplied by you.

All information used in these procedures was taken from details supplied by Terra Nova Financial.

As agreed we analyzed the information for the period from September 1, 2008 to April 30, 2009. Information for these months is considered to be relevant to the work performed.

The sufficiency of the procedures is the sole responsibility of Michael Parness. Consequently, we make no representations regarding questions or legal interpretation or the sufficiency of the procedures set out below for your purposes. Performance of these procedures by us should not supplant any additional inquiries or procedures you would undertake in your consideration of your trading activities gains/losses. This engagement to apply agreed-upon procedures was performed in accordance with the attestation standards established by the American Institute of Certified Public Accountants ("AICPA"). The procedures and findings are summarized below.

We were not engaged to, and did not conduct an audit or review, the objectives of which would be an expression of an opinion or limited assurance on the statements provided. Accordingly, we do not express such an opinion or limited assurance. Had we performed additional procedures, other matters might have come to our attention that would have been reported to you.

This report is intended solely for your information and is not intended and should not be used by any other unspecified party.

Cohen & Schaeffer P.C.

**New York, New York
June 17, 2010**

MICHAEL PARNESS
Agreed Upon Procedures

The agreed upon procedures that were performed and the related findings are as follows:

Procedure 1

Download copies of Terra Nova Financial – Account Statements of the Months of September 2008, October 2008, November 2008, December 2008, January 2009, February 2009, March 2009 and April 2009.

Procedure 2

Performed an analysis of the gains/losses as reported.

REALIZED GAINS OR LOSSES

	30-Sep	31-Oct	30-Nov	31-Dec	31-Jan	28-Feb	31-Mar	30-Apr	Total
Sales Proceeds	$ 52,621,169.35	$ 125,797,669.26	$ 253,655,409.23	$ 322,594,310.23	$ 282,145,450.43	$ 243,108,840.17	$ 445,239,447.59	$ 452,938,339.21	$ 2,178,100,635.47
Cost	52,148,226.21	125,357,562.62	252,501,019.88	322,028,564.87	281,749,224.78	242,442,344.24	445,222,660.66	452,800,927.74	2,174,250,531.00
Total Gains	$ 472,943.14	$ 440,106.64	$ 1,154,389.35	$ 565,745.36	$ 396,225.65	$ 666,495.93	$ 16,786.93	$ 137,411.47	$ 3,850,104.47

Procedure 3

Performed an analysis of funds.

ACTIVITY SUMMARY

	30-Sep	31-Oct	30-Nov	31-Dec	31-Jan	28-Feb	31-Mar	30-Apr	Total
Beginning funds	$ 12,822.88	$ 408,107.94	$ 270,678.60	$ 1,654,809.67	$ (137,326.56)	$ 9,797.06	$ 908,920.14	$ 461,385.05	12,822.88
Sec. purchased	(38,639,222.65)	(127,409,760.34)	(153,153,510.09)	(412,717,690.32)	(231,154,315.46)	(283,035,370.40)	(418,420,495.06)	(465,006,494.85)	(2,129,536,859.17)
Sec. sold	39,042,924.54	127,612,609.29	154,287,590.88	412,566,714.00	231,414,657.86	284,032,660.51	417,873,011.79	465,589,643.76	2,132,419,812.63
Funds deposited	88,250.00	179,700.00	250,000.00	43,030.00	287,000.00	402,000.00	100,000.00	313,000.00	1,662,980.00
Funds withdrawn	(101,650.00)	(520,000.00)		(1,700,030.00)	(400,000.00)	(500,000.00)		(500,000.00)	(3,721,680.00)
Other debits	(5,016.83)	(48.26)	(32.13)	(301.78)	(218.78)	(167.03)	(51.82)	(959.07)	(6,795.70)
Other credits	10,000.00	69.97	82.41	16,141.87					26,294.25
Ending Funds	$ 408,107.94	$ 270,678.60	$ 1,654,809.67	$ (137,326.56)	$ 9,797.06	$ 908,920.14	$ 461,385.05	$ 856,574.89	856,574.89

and in that time period every single rally was met with an at-times-violent crack back down even lower. Technically, we made what we term "lower highs and lower lows," meaning that when we did rally, the high of that rally was lower than the previous rallies' highs. The lows of the pullbacks were also lower than the previous pullbacks' lows. No matter what news came out, or how much buying investors did at any given point, selling was relentless.

The only people who made money were those willing and able to *short the market*. We shorted every rally and we shorted while we made lower lows.

For my style of trading, a *trending* market is best. It's how I've almost always done my best and shown my best profit. It could be trending higher, like when I made millions in 1999 and 2000, or it can be trending lower, like in 2008 and 2009. It doesn't matter to me, and it shouldn't ultimately matter to you.

To be fair, I'd rather the market trend up for myriad reasons, most importantly because more people make money when the market is going up than when it is going down. That's normal; people invest in the market, not that many short the market as an investment.

I also took a lot of chances, some of which I wouldn't recommend anyone do other than the most seasoned of traders. I used primarily options, and I also traded some futures. In order to make that much money over a short period of time, clearly I took some high risk/high reward trades. As I'm likely to mention several times in this book, and as I've mentioned thousands of times, if not tens of thousands of times in my career—*everything* in trading is *risk versus reward!*

If you are constantly taking trades where your downside is bigger than your upside, how do you think you're going to fare in the long run? Exactly! Not very well! So, you need to take trades where your risk is *well* defined and your reward is as large as possible. *But,* keep in mind this doesn't mean you start taking "crazy" shots, predicting stocks will go up 5,000 percent in a week, or even 100 percent in a month. Yes, there were/are times when I'll play highly speculative plays, but most of the times I'm looking for a 3-to-1 risk-versus-reward scenario. That is a *very* good place to be. Minimum is 1 to 1, but most of the trades I take are 2 or 3+ to 1 risk/reward. I want *you* to be in that range as well!

CHAPTER 6

Options (Pretty) Basic Primer

Most of my trades for many years now have been using *options.* Most of the Big Ka-chingos I've had over the years have been because of the leverage options provide. As you'll see, I'm not much of a scalper. I like the idea, and the reality that by using options I have a lot more control over my trading. For decades, investors heard the word *options* and thought it was like some evil spirit—"way too risky"—"fool's gold"—"gambling." They were right...and dead wrong. Like anything else related to the stock market, you can learn to use the tools the right way, or the wrong way. For those of you who are pros, consider this a refresher. For those of you who are newbies to the market, you should study and learn the ins and outs, the pros and cons of using options as part of your trading strategy.

I started almost solely using options after a day back in 2000 when I was short 10,000s of shares of some then high-flyers like Broadcom (BRCM), Juniper Networks (JNPR), CMGI (CMGI), and others. Then–Fed President Alan Greenspan announced a key rate decision intraday and I watched in horror (and spit up my chicken parmigiana hero on my keyboard) as I lost about $1,000,000 (yes, one million dollars!) and there was nothing I could do about it. Had I been using options, I would have still lost, but instead of an uncool million, I probably would have lost $100,000 or so...still a rough day at the office, but clearly a better alternative than adding another *zero* to the amount of pummeling I took.

This chapter provides a general overview of options, what they are, the definitions and terminology pertaining to options, and the basics of buying and selling options.

It's best to read the information contained in this chapter sequentially from the beginning to the end, since the concepts introduced later build on those introduced earlier. If you haven't had any exposure to options, your first introduction to the definitions and terminology surrounding options may seem a bit confusing or intimidating. Should a given topic not seem completely clear, I recommend that you continue reading through the remainder of the chapter. As you gain a broader perspective, the discussed concepts become easier to understand.

What Are Options?

An option is the right, but not the obligation, to buy or sell an underlying asset (stock, index, or other security) at a specified price on or before a specified date.

A *call* option is the right to buy the asset, and a *put* option is the right to sell (or for stocks, sell short) the asset. Whether it's a *call* or *put* option, the person who purchases the option is the *buyer*, and the person who originally sells the option is the *seller*.

Similar to buying a stock long or selling it short, you could buy a *call* option for a stock when you think the price is going higher, or a *put* option when you think the price is going to decline. If you are right in either case, you can potentially make money on the trade. However, unlike stocks, there is also a time-based value associated with trading options. In addition to gaining or losing value based upon the price of the underlying stock—an option can lose value over time. These issues, and others, related to trading options are covered in more detail later in this chapter, and in the next chapter.

Though the preceding definitions may make options seem somewhat mysterious and more complex to trade than stocks, they can actually be relatively simple to trade. Although it's possible to employ more complex option strategies, once you've learned the basics, you can also choose to simply buy and sell options in much the same way that you buy and sell stocks. You specify the desired option symbol, then buy at the best ask and sell at the best bid. Of course, just as with stocks, there are also risks associated with trading options. Therefore, before you actually begin trading options, you should understand both the pluses and minuses associated with trading them.

It's beyond the scope of this book to provide comprehensive information about all possible permutations of options trading. Instead, this book provides introductory options information in this chapter to help get you started, and then builds on it in the next chapter with practical techniques that I've actually used to profit from trading options. After reading the information provided here, if you would like to learn even more about options, there are numerous good books dedicated entirely to options. You can also visit www.AffinityTrading.com for a list of our recommended reading resources.

Options are commonly used for hedging, arbitrage plays, speculation, leverage, risk management, and more. However, options are also growing in popularity among active traders for other reasons. Active traders that are identified as pattern day traders are now subject to SEC regulations specifying minimum account funding requirements.

You are considered a pattern day trader if you trade in and out of stocks during the same day more than a certain number of times over a specified number of days. Since the specific requirements are subject to change, you can get the latest information about these requirements from your broker.

Currently, options aren't subject to the same regulations. Therefore, options provide a means for people to trade actively even when their account size would otherwise fall under the minimum requirements for pattern day traders. Again, check with your broker to ensure you have the current information; my experience is that some brokers have different definitions of the rules.

Another big advantage for people who fall into this category is the powerful leverage benefit associated with trading options. By trading options, traders with limited capital can still control a meaningful quantity of shares in a stock.

Underlying Assets

There are a variety of underlying assets for options, including the following examples:

- Stocks
- Indexes
- Commodities
- Futures

To simplify these descriptions, I'll refer to the underlying asset as stock, since stocks are the most popular form of options currently traded. Just keep in mind that the underlying asset could be indexes or other types of securities as well.

A stock option gives you the right to buy (*call* options) or sell (*put* options) 100 shares of the underlying stock at a specified price on or before a specified date. You also have the right to exercise stock options, that is, to take possession of the underlying stock. However, in most cases, traders simply sell the *call* or *put* options. It's less complicated and they usually have more value due to the way premiums are determined (more about this later). In the case of index options, you can't buy or sell actual indexes since they consist of more than one asset. Instead, you buy options that represent the value of the underlying assets. Each option represents 100 shares of the index. Some traders will occasionally buy index options like the S&P 100 (OEX), or others, to hedge other positions. Another potential use for index options is to quickly take advantage of an anticipated move in a sector or the overall market without taking the time to select an individual stock, or to spread risk among a collection of stocks.

Commodities options are for commodities such as corn, wheat, and so on. Since I don't use commodities and futures options as trading tools, I won't be discussing them in this book. I'm simply mentioning them in the interest of completeness and to let you know there are underlying option assets other than stocks.

Rights and Obligations

Buyer Rights

With options, all of the rights belong to the buyer. Buyers have the right to buy or sell short the underlying stock at the specified price on or before the expiration date.

Practically speaking, although they have the right to do so (and occasionally do), most options traders don't actually take possession of the underlying stock. Instead, they simply hold onto their options for a desired period of time, and similar to stocks, they sell the options, realizing any gains or losses accordingly. Or in some instances, the options may expire worthless.

Seller Obligations

All option obligations belong to the seller. The seller is obligated to provide the underlying stock. This applies to the original seller of the options (not to someone that purchases *calls* or *puts* and later sells them to close the position).

Once again, however, sellers rarely have to provide the actual underlying stock to the buyers. Still, buyers do occasionally exercise their options (more about this later), so sellers must be prepared to provide the stock, if required to do so.

Option Contracts

Option contracts consist of standardized terms that provide the rights (as described above) to buy or sell underlying stock. Option sellers are obligated to perform according to the contract terms. They must provide the underlying stock to the owner of the contract should the owner desire to exercise his or her options. There is more about this later under "Exercising Options."

You trade options by buying and/or selling one or more option contracts. Each contract represents the right to buy or sell short 100 shares of underlying stock. A working example of buying options is provided a bit later, under "Strike Price." For the moment, just keep in mind that an option contract represents 100 shares of the underlying stock.

Premium

Similar to paying a specific price when you buy a stock, you also pay a specific price when buying an option contract. The price of an option is called its *premium*. It's the price you pay for the right to buy or sell short shares of the underlying stock.

The premium is based on what is perceived to be the value of the option. A variety of factors go into determining the value of the premium. These are discussed later under "Intrinsic Value" and "Extrinsic Value."

The total cost of a contract is the premium multiplied by 100, since there are 100 shares of underlying stock per option contract (excluding broker commissions). A working example of this is provided in the following section.

Strike Price

When buying options, you pay a premium for the right to buy or sell short the underlying stock at a specific fixed price called the strike price. An example that illustrates this follows.

Option Price Examples

For purpose of illustration, Table 6.1 is a sample listing of *call* option price quotes for a hypothetical stock symbol called XYZ. However, the discussed concepts can be applied to any stock. The actual format for providing option price quotes varies from broker to broker. You can display options quotes using your own brokerage account to see how your particular broker displays the quotes.

The XYZ stock price is shown first. Beneath the stock's price are three *call* option quotes for the month of August. Note that only three quotes are shown below to conserve space and simplify this explanation, but many additional quotes are actually displayed when you access them through your broker. The next chapter, "Trading Options," provides additional examples of actual option price quote screens. A complete list of price quotes is sometimes referred to as an options *chain*.

Referencing the preceding example, the XYZ stock is currently selling for $46.00. Option symbols let you specify which options you want to trade in the same manner as stock ticker symbols let you specify stocks. The option symbols, which are sometimes a variation of the underlying stock's ticker symbol, change on a month-to-month basis. The strike prices for the three XYZ call options range from $42.50 to $47.50. The premiums, or last prices at which the options traded, range from $3.70 to $0.55. Notice the rate at which the premiums change the further they get away from the current XYZ stock price. How the premiums are determined is explained later. The current best bids, best asks, and volumes are also shown. Many brokers display, or provide the option to display, additional data as well. Once again, you can get information related to any additional option data from your specific broker.

Table 6.1 Option Price Quotes for XYZ

Stock	Price	Bid	Ask	Last	Volume
XYZ	46.00	45.95	46.02	46.00	10,284,561

XYZ July-15-Calls

Symbol	Price	Bid	Ask	Last	Volume
XOEHV	42.50	3.50	3.80	3.70	428
XOEHI	45.00	1.75	1.80	1.75	789
XOEHW	47.50	0.45	0.55	0.55	1047

In this case, if you wanted to buy 10 July XYZ CALL options (contracts), according to the asking price of $1.80, you would pay $1800, less commission charges. To derive the total, you multiply 1.80 by 100 shares per contract by 10 contracts ($1.80 × 100 × 10 = $1800).

Expiration Date/Month

Monthly options expire on the third Saturday of each month; however, the last day for trading them is the third Friday. You choose the desired expiration month when you purchase an option.

For example, the expiration month shown in the preceding example is July, but you could also purchase options for September or October. You can even purchase long-term option contracts, called a LEAP. LEAPs are any option that is nine months or more away from the current expiration month. The greater the time until expiration, the higher is the time-based portion of the premium (explained below under "Extrinsic Value").

If the *call* or *put* options you buy expire without "value," then they expire worthless, and you lose the entire premium. However, your original premium is the most that you can lose. Though many brokers *sell* options on the expiration day and deposit any proceeds into your account, some may not. In this case, you may need to sell options that have value on or before the expiration date. Check with your broker to find out how they handle option expirations.

Weekly Options

In recent years, weekly option contracts have become increasingly popular. I trade a lot of weekly options, as I like the flexibility of choosing to roll my trade over to the next week (or month), or selling out of the position. The premiums are obviously going to be less if I hold an option on a stock for a week versus a month versus a year. The same general rules apply to weekly versus monthly options; you just get less time to hold the position.

Intrinsic Value

The *intrinsic value* of an option is the difference between the underlying stock price and the strike price of the option. For example, if the stock price of XYZ was $55 and you bought a $50 *call* option, the intrinsic value would be $5 ($55 − $50 = $5). Therefore, when the underlying stock price of a *call* option climbs higher than the strike price, the intrinsic value (and premium) of the option goes up accordingly.

The intrinsic value for *call* options can only be a positive number or zero. If the calculations come out negative, then the value is considered zero. For example, if the XYZ stock price was $50 and the *call* option was $55, the intrinsic value would be zero ($50 − $55 = −$5 = 0).

Conversely, the opposite is true for *put* options. The intrinsic value of *put* options can only be negative (however, the negative sign is dropped). And, any positive numbers are considered to have a zero value.

Extrinsic Value

The portion of an option premium that is not intrinsic value is extrinsic value. Extrinsic value is determined by a complex standardized formula based on time and *volatility* (covered next). Extrinsic value is predominately a time-based value, or a time premium. It's based primarily on the length of time that remains before an option expires. As the time to expiration decreases, the extrinsic value decreases.

Volatility

Volatility is a measure of how fast the underlying stock changes price. A stock that has wide price swings in a relatively short period of time is considered to be more volatile than one whose price changes only a small amount or very slowly over time.

As just mentioned, the volatility of the underlying stock is reflected to some degree in an option's premium. Higher volatility causes the volatility portion of an option's premium to be higher. In this regard, there are essentially two types of volatility that come into play, *historical volatility* and *implied volatility*.

Historical Volatility

Historical volatility is a statistical measure of volatility for a specific amount of time (e.g., 10 days, 100 days, or another desired time period).

Implied Volatility

Implied volatility is a measure of the option market's perception of what volatility will likely be in the future.

In the Money

An option that has intrinsic value is said to be *in the money*. For a *call* option, this occurs when the underlying stock price is greater than the strike price. The opposite is true for *put* options. A *put* option has intrinsic value when the underlying stock price is less than the strike price.

For example, a $50 XYZ *call* option would be in the money by $5 if the XYZ stock price were $55. A $50 XYZ *put* option would be in the money by $5 if the XYZ stock price were $45.

Out of the Money

A *call* option is out of the money when the underlying stock price is less than the strike price, or greater than the stock price in the case of *puts*. In this case, it has no intrinsic value—that is, the intrinsic value is zero.

For example, a $50 XYZ *call* option would be out of the money by $5 if the XYZ stock price were $45. A $50 XYZ *put* option would be out of the money by $5 if the XYZ stock price were $55.

An option that is out of the money has only extrinsic value, or time-based value, which decreases as the option nears its expiration date. The option could expire worthless if it reaches its expiration date without any intrinsic value.

At the Money

An option is at the money when its underlying stock price is equal to its strike price. For example, a $50 XYZ *call* or *put* option is at the money when the XYZ stock price is $50.

Hedging

You can use options to preserve gains, or reduce losses, on an open stock position without selling your stock. This is called hedging.

For example, if the market appears weak, you might buy *puts* on your open stock position. If your stock drops in value, the *puts* will go up in value and help offset any losses. Additional information about hedging is provided the next chapter, "Trading Options."

Managing Risk

Options are a great way to predefine your maximum risk on a trade, or to limit your overall risk exposure. Though you could lose the entire premium if an option expires worthless, you cannot lose more than the premium. Therefore, your maximum possible losses can be easily determined in advance based on the total cost of the options. I particularly like this aspect of trading options and will be discussing it more in the next chapter.

Speculation and Leverage

If you feel a stock is going up or down in value but aren't certain, or if you want to leverage your money so you can control a larger quantity of shares with a predetermined amount of risk, you can accomplish either by purchasing *call* or *put* options.

I will frequently speculate using options to limit risk when I think a stock has the potential to make a large move, particularly at times the risk/reward for a trade is favorable, and the option premiums are reasonable. Using options to speculate on earnings trends is one example.

As I mentioned earlier, options are also great for leveraging your money. For example, referring back to the prior quotes example, if you wanted to buy 1000 shares of the XYZ stock and it is selling for $46, it would cost you $46,000. However, you could control 1000 shares of the stock by buying 10 in-the-money *call* option contracts. You would buy the $45 *call* options at the asking price of $1.80 per contract for a total cost of only $1800. Now, that's leverage!

Arbitrage

Sophisticated traders can take advantage of price discrepancies between two underlying assets (such as two different options on different exchanges). This process is called *arbitrage.*

Options Pros and Cons

The main pros associated with options trading are leveraging, hedging, and predefining risk. You can leverage your available funds by paying a small price to control a large amount of stock for a larger potential gain; you can hedge outstanding stock positions against loss without giving up your original positions; and you can earn gains using low-risk option strategies where the maximum risk is known in advance.

Another advantage to trading options is that unlike stocks, options aren't subject to the SEC regulation that applies to pattern day traders, which requires the maintenance of a $25,000 account balance for traders who trade in and out of positions more than four times during any consecutive five-day time period. (Check with your broker.)

A major drawback to options is their time-based value. Although stocks never expire, if there is no intrinsic value remaining, options expire at a specific date and become worthless. Time is your enemy when you own options. When you own stock, your enemy is being married to the equity.

Volume

Similar to stocks, you can check option volume by the day, week, month, and so on.

You can watch for volume increases and decreases over a given time period and compare the amount of change to the average volume. If the volume is increasing, then there may be something of interest going on that could put pressure on the value of the option. I'll discuss volume and liquidity more in Chapter 7 under "Index Options."

Open Interest

Open interest is a running measure of the number of option contracts that have been opened. For example, when trading options, you must buy or sell to open a position. Open interest tracks the total number of open contracts. Subsequently, when you sell to close a position, the amount of open interest decreases.

Don't confuse open interest with volume. Volume could be up as a result of traders repeatedly trading in and out of positions, while open interest reflects how many contracts are actually open. High open interest indicates a large number of people are trading the options.

Exercising Options

With American options, as opposed to European, you can exercise your rights to take possession of the underlying stock at any time on or before the expiration date. The seller is obligated to provide the underlying stock.

Since you can simply trade in and out of options like stock, most options traders never actually exercise their options. Because of the added extrinsic value (time value), the options are usually worth more than the underlying stock alone. If a situation arises where this isn't the case, or you simply want to own the underlying stock, you can choose to exercise your options and take possession of the stock.

If you don't sell or exercise an option by the time it expires, most brokers sell the option and deposit any proceeds into your account.

However, since brokers all determine their own policies, you should check with your broker for the specifics about how they handle option expirations.

Option Strategies Introduction

Buying Calls and Puts

As mentioned previously, you might buy *calls* and *puts* for a variety of reasons, ranging from leveraging your money to hedging to pre-defining your risk on a trade.

If you feel a stock is going up, you could buy the stock and hold it, or you could buy *call* options. If you think a stock is going down, you could short the stock, or you could buy *put* options. Alternatively, if the market appears weak and you are holding a position in a stock that you don't want to sell, you could buy *puts* as a hedge. If your stock price declines, the *puts* will go up in value and help reduce losses. The amount of protection you receive depends on the strike price you choose for the options.

The closer an option is to being in the money, the more expensive it is due to both intrinsic and extrinsic values coming into play together.

Once an option is in the money, it gains intrinsic value dollar for dollar with the stock price. Conversely, when an option is out of the money, it's less expensive because it has no intrinsic value. The extrinsic value also plays a role. Since extrinsic value is time based, the closer an option is to expiring, the less the extrinsic value.

Unlike stocks, your predefined risk is limited to the total premium you pay for the options. In the example previously used, if you bought 1000 shares of the XYZ stock for $46, the total cost would be $46,000 (excluding commissions). Though unlikely, if the company abruptly went out of business, you could hypothetically lose your entire $46,000 investment. Alternatively, if you bought 10 $45 *call* options at $1.80 each for a total of $1800 (excluding commissions), the most you could lose is the $1800 premium. Of course, in either case, you should further limit your maximum risk exposure by also using stop-loss orders.

To determine which option best suits your needs, you need to consider the purpose of the option along with its premium costs. Do you want an option that is in the money at a higher cost or out of the money at a lower cost? Do you want an option that is nearing its expiration date at a lower cost or one that isn't close to expiring at a higher cost?

In Chapter 7, I'll provide examples and discuss other ways you can consider trading options.

Selling Naked Calls and Puts

If the original seller of *calls* or *puts* does not own the underlying stock, then it's called selling *naked*. This is riskier than simply buying or selling *calls* and *puts*.

Note: Selling *calls* or *puts* to close a position you bought is not the same thing as being the original seller that I'm discussing here, that is, the person who sells to open a position rather than to close a position.

You must have an options margin account to sell *naked calls* and *puts*. Selling *naked* is what the pros do when the implied volatility gets very high and the premium is overvalued. When selling *naked*, the risk is virtually unlimited while the reward is limited to the premium.

In this case, time works for you, unlike buying *calls* or *puts*, where time works against you. You want the options to expire so you can collect the premiums.

Here are examples that illustrate the risk/reward. If the XYZ stock price is $50 and you buy a single XYZ $55 *call* contract at $2, the most you can lose is $200 ($2 × 100 shares). If you sell an XYZ $55 *call naked*, the most you can collect is $200 when XYZ is $55 or under. If, however, XYZ runs to $70, you would lose $15 ($70 − $55) times 100 shares, minus the premium, or $1300. Since the XYZ stock price could theoretically go even higher, the potential loss could get worse accordingly.

Selling Covered Calls and Puts

If the original seller of *calls* or *puts* owns the underlying stock, then it is called selling covered. In this case, the seller must own the same number of shares that are being sold as *calls* or *puts*. As previously noted, selling your *calls* or *puts* to close a position is not the same thing as being the original seller that is referred to here—that is, the person who sells to open a position rather than to close a position.

Selling covered *calls* is a good way to earn income on stocks with prices that are essentially moving sideways or rising only slightly. It's approved for most option IRA accounts, and you can also do it with *puts* (but not in IRAs) by selling short the stock and selling an equal number of *puts*.

When selling covered *calls* and *puts*, the risk is limited and the reward is the premium you collect. If the stock goes down, you get to collect the premium on the covered *call* but your original investment in the stock loses value, which is why it's best suited to stocks where the price is basically flat or slightly increasing. As with selling *naked calls* and *puts*, time works for you. You want the option to expire so you can collect the premium.

Here is an example that illustrates the risk/reward. Say you sell an XYZ $55 covered *call* and own an equal amount of the stock. If XYZ rallies to $70, even though you are out $15 on the *call*, you made $20 on the stock—so you are covered.

Spreads

A *spread* refers to buying one option and selling another at a different strike price.

With bull spreads, you buy an option and sell another one at a price that is a strike price, or a few strike prices, higher than the one you bought, and then you collect the premium. This lowers your risk to the amount you paid for the option you bought, minus the premium you collected from the one you sold. The reward is limited since it falls between the two strike prices. However, even though the profits are limited, the risk is much lower as well.

For example, suppose you buy our hypothetical stock's XYZ $55 *calls* at $3 and sell XYZ $60 *calls* for $1. The net out-of-pocket cost is $2 ($3 − $1). If XYZ is $60 or above by the expiration date, the most you can make is $5, the difference between the $60 *calls* you sold and the $55 *calls* you bought, less the $2 net out-of-pocket cost for the options, which results in a maximum profit potential of $3. If XYZ is $55 or less at expiration, the most you can lose is the $2 out-of-pocket cost.

You can do the same thing with a bear spread by buying *puts* and reversing the process. Additional information about bull and bear spreads is provided in the next chapter.

CHAPTER

7

Trading Options

This chapter expands on many of the concepts introduced in Chapter 6. If you are new to options and haven't yet read the preceding chapter, or if you simply need a refresher concerning option definitions and terminology, please review the previous chapter.

It's important to keep in mind that the techniques described here are speculative plays, which is why I typically qualify them as such whenever I send out applicable option email alerts. Though you can frequently achieve nice gains, you shouldn't get carried away on these trades since they are inherently speculative in nature.

Out-of-the-Money Options

As explained in the preceding chapter, a *call* option is out of the money when the underlying stock's price is less than the option's strike price, or in the case of *puts*, when the underlying stock's price is greater than the option's strike price.

Figure 7.1 is an options quote screen for KLAC for the month of December. The options expire for trading on the third Friday during the month of December. The current stock price for KLAC is $42.85. Note that the quote screen shown here is for illustration purposes only. Actual screen formats and layouts vary among trading platforms.

Looking at Figure 7.1, under the "Title" column the *call* options that are $45 and higher are all out-of-the-money options since they are higher than the $42.85 KLA-Tencor (KLAC) stock price. Alternatively, the *call* options that are $40 and under are all in the money.

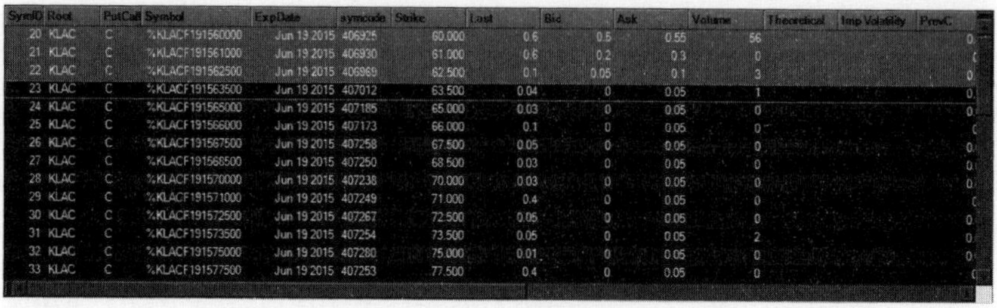

SymID Root	PutCall	Symbol	ExpDate	symcode	Strike	Last	Bid	Ask	Volume	Theoretical	Imp Volatility	PrvC
20 KLAC	C	%KLACF191560000	Jun 13 2015	406925	60.000	0.6	0.5	0.55	56			0
21 KLAC	C	%KLACF191561000	Jun 13 2015	406930	61.000	0.6	0.2	0.3	0			
22 KLAC	C	%KLACF191562500	Jun 13 2015	406969	62.500	0.1	0.05	0.1	3			0
23 KLAC	C	%KLACF191563500	Jun 19 2015	407012	63.500	0.04	0	0.05	1			0
24 KLAC	C	%KLACF191565000	Jun 19 2015	407185	65.000	0.03	0	0.05	0			0
25 KLAC	C	%KLACF191566000	Jun 19 2015	407173	66.000	0.1	0	0.05	0			
26 KLAC	C	%KLACF191567500	Jun 19 2015	407258	67.500	0.05	0	0.05	0			0
27 KLAC	C	%KLACF191568500	Jun 19 2015	407250	68.500	0.03	0	0.05	0			0
28 KLAC	C	%KLACF191570000	Jun 19 2015	407238	70.000	0.03	0	0.05	0			0
29 KLAC	C	%KLACF191571000	Jun 19 2015	407249	71.000	0.4	0	0.05	0			
30 KLAC	C	%KLACF191572500	Jun 19 2015	407267	72.500	0.05	0	0.05	0			0
31 KLAC	C	%KLACF191573500	Jun 19 2015	407254	73.500	0.05	0	0.05	2			0
32 KLAC	C	%KLACF191575000	Jun 19 2015	407280	75.000	0.01	0	0.05	0			0
33 KLAC	C	%KLACF191577500	Jun 19 2015	407253	77.500	0.4	0	0.05	0			

Figure 7.1   Options Quote Screen for KLAC

Conversely, the *put* options that are $40 and under are out of the money, since they are lower than the $42.85 KLAC stock price, and the *put* options that are $45 and above are in the money.

Notice that the further out of the money an option is, the cheaper it costs. See the "Last" price column in the preceding example. The $40 in-the-money *call* option last traded at $4.40 while the $45 out-of-the-money *call* last traded at $1.70. Though the option costs are lower, trading out-of-the-money options is more speculative because the stock's price has to move farther to hit the option strike price (e.g., the $45 strike price, in this case).

Regardless, trading options that are somewhat out of the money is a great way to trade momentum stocks with limited, predefined risk. For example, if you thought KLAC was going to have a big move up in the near future but you weren't sure or you just wanted to precisely define your maximum risk exposure, rather than buying the stock, you could buy the $45 KLAC *call* options at $1.75 (the current asking price shown for the $45 *call* in the preceding illustration).

If you held the options until expiration, to make money the KLAC stock price would need to rise above $46.75 (the $45 option strike price plus your $1.75 option premium/cost). Your maximum risk, if the stock price remains below the $45 option strike price, is the $1.75 option cost (multiplied by 100 shares per contract, or $170.50 plus commissions per option contract). If, at options expiration, the KLAC stock price were between $45 and $46.75, it would defray some of the option costs and lessen your losses accordingly. For example, if the stock's price were $45.50 when the options expired, you would lose $1.25 per contract share rather than the original $1.75 cost. The closer options get to expiration, the lower the time-based value of the options, so at expiration the value is determined by the intrinsic value, based on the difference between the option price and the stock price.

Of course, the prior examples apply to holding options through expiration. Often, except possibly for very cheap or small "all or nothing" option plays, you sell your options prior to expiration. Just like when a stock trade goes against you, rather than waiting for it to fall to zero, you can sell the stock at the time of your choosing. Or, you can take profits at any time. Similarly, you can do the same with options, assuming the options you have chosen are reasonably liquid and someone is available to take the other side of the trade. Additionally, you can potentially limit losses by using stop-losses on option plays as well.

Using the preceding example again, if the KLAC stock price went to $45 rather than $46.75 or higher, rather than holding your *call* options through expiration, you could sell them for a very nice profit.

You could even potentially double your money. If KLAC went from $42.85 to $45, you would mostly likely get over $3.00 for the $1.75 *call* options you purchased, which would be a nice trade indeed!

We have actually achieved similar results playing options on momentum stocks during earnings season. A recent example is PMCS.

We played the MAY $7.50 *call* options at $0.35 for an earnings run when the stock price was around $6.90. Brocade (BRCD), which is in a similar industry, had recently reported positive earnings and the stock responded quite favorably. As a result, PMC-Sierra (PMCS) seemed like a good risk/reward speculative play for options. To make money on the trade, we needed the stock price to break $7.85 ($7.50 + $0.35 option premium). The price subsequently moved up to a range of $7.90 to $8.00, which took the options to $0.70 for a short-term double!

As I mentioned, historically speaking, options are a great way to speculate on momentum stocks such as the Internet, and Biotech stocks (GOOG, AAPL, FB, RGEN, GILD, EBAY, EXPE, etc.) when you anticipate a strong near-term move. I particularly like playing options during earnings season, when prices tend to be more volatile. I'll discuss this more later.

Similar to speculating with *call* options, if you think a stock's price is going down rather than up, you can buy *put* options. As when shorting stocks, you want the underlying stock price to go lower after buying the *put* options.

Referring to the prior illustration again, you could play the KLAC $40 out-of-the-money *puts* for roughly the same price as the $45 *calls*, or $1.70 (see the best ask column). Notice that the $42.85 KLAC stock price is near the midpoint between the $40 *puts* and the $45 *calls*, meaning both the *calls* and *puts* are a similar distance out of the money, which resulted in a comparable option premium for both.

To make money on the $40 KLAC *put* options, you need the stock's price to move toward the $40 option strike price near term, or below $40 by option expiration. If the stock's price stays substantially the same over time, or until the options expire, the time-based portion of the option premium will decline, resulting in a loss on the trade.

Figure 7.2 is another December options quote screen for EXPE. The current EXPE stock price is $75.08.

Looking at Figure 7.2, notice that both the stock price and the option premiums are considerably higher than those for the preceding KLAC example. Additionally, EXPE tends to be more volatile and trades in larger price ranges than KLAC. As explained in the preceding chapter, volatility is also a factor in calculating the extrinsic, time-based component of an option's premium. To some degree, this is reflected in the higher option premiums for EXPE. See the $4.30 and $4.20 premiums for the $75 EXPE *calls* and *puts*, respectively, in Figure 7.2.

In this case, to play options that are out of the money, you would need to go about $5.00 out of the money. For example, the $80 EXPE *call* options are $2.05, which is more expensive than the $45 *call* options at $1.75 in the preceding KLAC example. Even though the EXPE options are further out of the money, the premiums are higher.

In this case, if you bought the EXPE $80 *call* options at $2.05, the EXPE stock price would need to move from $75.08 to above $82.05 (the $80 option strike price plus the $2.05 premium) in order to make money at the time the options expire. However, once again, you could still potentially make money prior to option expiration, if the EXPE stock price moves sufficiently higher in a sufficiently short

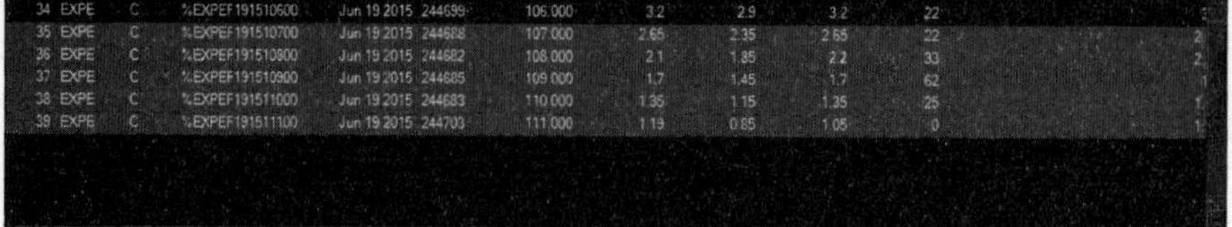

SymID Root	PutCall	Symbol	ExpDate		Strike	Last	Bid	Ask	Volume	Theoretical	Imp Volatility	PrcyC
30 EXPE	C	%EXPEF191510200	Jun 19 2015	244721	102.000	10	5.7	6.1	0			
31 EXPE	C	%EXPEF191510300	Jun 19 2015	244723	103.000	6.5	4.9	5.3	10			
32 EXPE	C	%EXPEF191510400	Jun 19 2015	244715	104.000	8.54	4.1	4.6	0			8.
33 EXPE	C	%EXPEF191510500	Jun 19 2015	244686	105.000	3.8	3.5	3.8	31			4
34 EXPE	C	%EXPEF191510500	Jun 19 2015	244699	106.000	3.2	2.9	3.2	22			
35 EXPE	C	%EXPEF191510700	Jun 19 2015	244688	107.000	2.65	2.35	2.65	22			2
36 EXPE	C	%EXPEF191510800	Jun 19 2015	244682	108.000	2.1	1.85	2.2	33			2
37 EXPE	C	%EXPEF191510900	Jun 19 2015	244685	109.000	1.7	1.45	1.7	62			
38 EXPE	C	%EXPEF191511000	Jun 19 2015	244683	110.000	1.35	1.15	1.35	25			1.
39 EXPE	C	%EXPEF191511100	Jun 19 2015	244703	111.000	1.19	0.85	1.05	0			1.

Figure 7.2   December Options Quote Screen for EXPE

period of time. For example, if EXPE moved up by $3.00 the day after you bought the options for $2.05, considering the volatility, your options would likely be worth over $3.00. If desired, you could sell them (or a portion of them, which is what I frequently do) at this point for a nice profit.

The potential rewards of this type of scenario, along with the limited predefined risk, is one of the reasons I like speculating with options when I anticipate the possibility of a large near-term price move. Since momentum stocks tend to be volatile and make large moves during earnings season due to the earnings runs, earnings warnings, breaking news, upgrades/downgrades, and so on, this is a great time to speculate using options.

However, using the previous example, if you held the options rather than taking profits, the time-based premium would continue to decrease at an ever-accelerating rate as the option expiration date approached. Unless the stock price continued moving higher, you would eventually not only lose your prior gains, you would also lose your original premium. If the stock price didn't move higher, the premiums would decrease to the point that the options would be worthless by the time they expired. During the final week prior to expiration, the preceding premiums would be considerably lower. If the EXPE stock price didn't change substantially, the premiums would likely be worth around $1.00 or $1.25 during the final week of option expirations. This illustrates the risk associated with options. If the underlying stock's price doesn't move in your favor, depending on the time until expiration, you can potentially lose your original premium at a rapid rate.

Some of the best opportunities are presented during the final week of option expirations. Due to the lower premium costs, I particularly like trading options for companies that are scheduled to report earnings at this time. The anticipated earnings reports help generate the needed volatility for large near-term price moves, and by using options, you can precisely predefine your maximum risk exposure in the event a trade goes against you.

More than One Month Out

It's also possible to buy options with an expiration date that is further out than the current month. For example, instead of buying December options like in the prior EXPE illustration, you could buy

January or February options, or options where the expiration date is even further out.

As you might expect, however, the longer the time period is before expiration, the higher the option premiums, and the greater the risk. I generally buy options for the current month as short-term trades.

However, there are occasions when it could make sense to consider options that are further out than the current month. For example, you might want to consider buying the following month's options when the expiration date for the current month is close (a few days to a week away), and you anticipate a stock is going to have a large price move but you can't be certain it will occur prior to the current month's expiration date.

Figure 7.3 shows the option price quotes for ERTS, which are more than a month away from expiration. These quotes were obtained during the month of December for options that expire during the month of March.

The current stock price is $67.18.

Notice in the preceding illustration that the premium of the $70 *call* option is $5.50 at the best ask, which is quite a hefty premium.

Considering the option is also $2.82 out of the money ($70 minus the $67.18 stock price), the total effective premium is actually $8.32 (the $5.50 cost plus the $2.82 out-of-the-money amount). If you were holding the options for the long run, you would need a substantial price move in your favor to come out on the trade.

As I discussed previously, I rarely make this type of long-term option trade; however, there could be an occasional instance when I might consider it. For example, maybe there is a rumor that ERTS is going to be bought out or there's some other catalyst that could potentially propel the price higher over the next few months.

Symbl	Root	PutCall	Symbol	ExpDate	symonde	Strike	Last	Bid	Ask	Volume	Theoretical	Imp Volatility	Prev C
48	EA	C	%EAF191559500	Jun 19 2015	202462	59.500	0	3.85	4.25	0			
49	EA	C	%EAF191560000	Jun 19 2015	202427	60.000	3.8	3.45	3.8	4			3
50	EA	C	%EAF191560500	Jun 19 2015	202408	60.500	2.68	3.15	3.3	0			2
51	EA	C	%EAF191561000	Jun 19 2015	202400	61.000	3.2	2.73	2.87	0			
52	EA	C	%EAF191561500	Jun 19 2015	202387	61.500	2.07	2.37	2.56	0			2
53	EA	C	%EAF191562000	Jun 15 2015	202390	62.000	1.81	2.05	2.12	0			1
54	EA	C	%EAF191562500	Jun 19 2015	202386	62.500	1.66	1.71	1.78	6			1
55	EA	C	%EAF191563000	Jun 19 2015	202385	63.000	1.39	1.4	1.48	0			1
56	EA	C	%EAF191563500	Jun 19 2015	202393	63.500	1.19	1.14	1.19	41			1
57	EA	C	%EAF191564000	Jun 19 2015	202339	64.000	0.97	0.93	0.96	42			0
58	EA	C	%EAF191564500	Jun 19 2015	202402	64.500	0.73	0.71	0.77	0			0
59	EA	C	%EAF191565000	Jun 19 2015	202410	65.000	0.65	0.55	0.61	2			0

Figure 7.3   Option Price Quotes for ERTS

In instances such as these, speculating with options that are further than the current month out could be justified.

However, if I were to make this type of trade, I would likely buy in-the-money options rather than out-of-the-money options. Instead of buying the $70 *call*, I might buy the $60 *call* at the current $11.30 asking price. At first glance, this seems more expensive, but the total cost is actually less. The $60 strike price plus $11.30 is $71.30, while the $70 strike price plus $5.50 is $75.50. And, the $60 *call* is already in the money. The $70 *call* costs you $4.20 more to go further out of the money.

When buying options, I strongly encourage you to use only limit orders rather than market orders. Often, options are less liquid than stocks and they tend to have larger price spreads. Using limit orders helps ensure your order will fill according to your plan for the trade, rather than leaving you open to a potentially unfavorable price that's determined by a market maker.

Leveraging and Hedging

As I discussed in Chapter 6, you can also buy *calls* and *puts* to preserve gains or to reduce potential losses on your existing stock positions. This is referred to as hedging. You would buy *puts* to hedge long positions against losses, and *calls* to hedge short positions.

The relative importance of using hedges tends to correspond to how leveraged your account is, and its size. If you have a large account that is heavily leveraged (e.g., with a high percentage of positions leaning in the same direction, either long or short), then it is more important to consider hedging your account to protect against excessive losses should the market unexpectedly move against you.

For example, suppose you are holding large positions in stocks that you don't want to sell. Maybe you feel the stocks have more upside potential but the market overall appears to be weakening. To guard against potential losses, you could buy *puts* as a hedge. If your stocks' prices decline, the *puts* will go up in value and help reduce losses on your long positions. The amount of protection you receive depends on the options you choose and their resulting premiums, and how many options you buy.

As you might expect, there is a price to pay for the protection achieved from hedging. If a stock's price goes up, although you will gain on the stock, you will lose money on the *put* options, which reduces your overall gains accordingly. Still, if you have a large number of open stock positions that you intend to hold overnight or longer, it's a good idea to guard against a large loss from adverse news, or for whatever reason, by using a reasonable amount of hedging. If you had a $300,000 portfolio heavily leveraged on the long side, you don't want to wake up the next morning to a $40,000 loss due to unexpected bad news.

You could potentially hedge your entire portfolio against all losses, or you could simply hedge to reduce or limit your overall risk exposure.

If your account is heavily leveraged on the long side, it implies that you are bullish and believe the market is going higher. Since your bias is to the upside, you would generally want to maintain that bias and rather than attempting to cover your entire portfolio against a downside move, you would just hedge sufficiently to limit your overall risk exposure in a worse-case scenario, or in the event you are wrong about the direction of the market. With this approach, although you would still lose money, you wouldn't suffer an excessive loss or get wiped out if the market had a large move contrary to your heavily leveraged account.

In most cases, to help keep the cost of hedging within reason "traders" would only hedge on a short-term basis to temporarily limit losses rather than to protect against all possible losses, or rather than hedging over a long period of time. Since I'm a trader and rarely hold positions for a long time period, if I hedge at all, the duration of my hedging is typically less than a week, and most of my hedges last only one to three days. I don't want to lose too much of the time-based value on option premiums. Also, since there is usually an expense associated with hedging, I generally employ hedging techniques only in cases where I have sizable positions that I'm holding overnight and limiting losses by other means, such as with stop losses or smaller lot sizes, may not be sufficient.

There are a variety of other methods you could consider using to hedge your account. Rather than buying *puts* for specific long positions that you are holding, you could consider hedging with other stocks that appear weaker than the stocks you are holding long, or you might use index options to hedge against your entire portfolio. See the "Index Options" section for more about these. Additionally, you could consider taking short positions in weak stocks or the overall market as a hedge rather than using options. In an ideal scenario, you might even achieve profits on both your long positions and your hedges, though for obvious reasons, this isn't the typical outcome. Still, I've had many instances where I was holding long positions and used weaker stocks or the overall market as a hedge, and realized gains on both.

Since there is considerable flexibility in the approaches you can take to hedge, the best approach depends on your own personal objectives and preferences, the specific circumstances, the size of your account, and your own tolerance for risk. If you don't have a large account, then it's probably best simply to manage risk by other means rather than employ hedging strategies. As I've frequently commented, you should always use stop losses to limit your potential losses whenever possible, and you can adjust lot sizes to reduce your risk exposure.

In cases where this may be less practical, as with particularly large positions or large heavily leveraged portfolios, hedging can be a useful alternative.

Index Options

There are times when you might find it more convenient to trade index options rather than individual stock options.

If you anticipate a pending sector or general market move and would like to react quickly without taking the time to pick specific stocks, you can do so by using index options. For example, if positive news came out about semiconductor stocks and you needed to act quickly, you could consider buying *call* options for the Semiconductor Index (SOX) rather than trying to pick among individual semiconductor stocks.

Of course, you can always consider buying the index long, rather than using options, but since many of the indexes are very expensive, using options is a more affordable alternative. As I'll illustrate in a moment, index option premiums can be expensive as well, but due to the leverage provided by options, they are considerably cheaper than buying the index itself. Still, the cost of some index options may make trading them impractical for traders with smaller account sizes. Buying options for exchange-traded funds (ETFs), or holders, such as SMH, BBH, GLD, and so on are another possibility you can consider.

Index options or ETFs can also be used to reduce overall risk exposure by spreading risk across the collection of companies that make up the index. And, as I discussed under "Leverage and Hedging," you can use index options to hedge your entire portfolio against potential losses.

Additionally, I've frequently used index options to play other trends such as earnings trends or the FOMC runs described in Chapter 13.

Figure 7.4 shows December option quotes for SOX. At the time of these quotes, SOX was priced at $362.64.

Due to their cost and the rapidly declining value of the time-based portion of the premiums, I generally only use index options for relatively short-term trades, possibly up to a week or so but preferably, only one or two days. For example, notice the premiums for the $365 *call* options in the preceding illustration. The best bid is $20.80 and the best ask is $23.80. Though it's much less than the $362.64 index cost, it is still an expensive option.

Although these options are expensive, one of the things that I like about them is they tend to move in fairly large increments in a short time frame whenever the market moves, unlike individual stocks where it can be less certain whether you'll get a $0.50 or $1.00 move out of them when the market moves, index options are likely to move dramatically.

Of course, since a move could go against you, you should take into consideration that your losses can mount up quickly as well.

A significant disadvantage to these options is the size of the spread.

Looking at the bids and asks on the previous quote screen, you can see that there is about a $2.00 to $3.00 difference, or premium, between them in most cases. For example, there is a $3.00 difference between the bid and ask of the $365 *call* discussed earlier ($23.80 − $20.80 = $3.00).

SymID	Root	PutCall	Symbol	ExpDate	symcode	Strike	Last	Bid	Ask	Volume	Theoretical	Imp Volatility	PrevC
20	SMH	C	%SMHF191555000	Jun 19 2015	359784	55.000	2.9	3.4	3.9	0			
21	SMH	C	%SMHF191556000	Jun 19 2015	359724	56.000	3.09	2.65	2.75	0			3
22	SMH	C	%SMHF191557000	Jun 19 2015	359710	57.000	1.9	1.8	1.95	11			2
23	SMH	C	%SMHF191558000	Jun 19 2015	359711	58.000	1.2	1.1	1.25	13			1
24	SMH	C	%SMHF191559000	Jun 19 2015	359713	59.000	0.65	0.6	0.65	20			0
25	SMH	C	%SMHF191560000	Jun 19 2015	359716	60.000	0.3	0.25	0.3	3			0
26	SMH	C	%SMHF191561000	Jun 19 2015	359743	61.000	0.25	0.1	0.15	0			0
27	SMH	C	%SMHF191562000	Jun 19 2015	359770	62.000	0.23	0	0.1	0			0
28	SMH	C	%SMHF191563000	Jun 19 2015	359850	63.000	0.1	0	0.05	0			0
29	SMH	C	%SMHF191564000	Jun 19 2015	360039	64.000	0.05	0	0.05	0			0
30	SMH	C	%SMHF191565000	Jun 19 2015	360037	65.000	0.03	0	0.05	0			0
31	SMH	C	%SMHF191566000	Jun 19 2015	360027	66.000	0	0	0.05	0			
32	SMH	C	%SMHF191567000	Jun 19 2015	360073	67.000	0	0	0.05	0			
33	SMH	C	%SMHF191568000	Jun 19 2015	360098	68.000	0	0	0.05	0			

Figure 7.4   December Option Quotes for SOX

The size of the spread lessens as you get further out of the money, but even then the premiums are substantial. If you were to open a position and subsequently changed your mind, you could potentially lose 10 percent to 15 percent by simply getting out of the trade.

As I touched on earlier, when trading options I recommend using only limit orders. Though some options have a fairly high degree of liquidity, many are thinly traded. Considering the lower liquidity and wider spreads, you could receive very unfavorable fills using market orders. Though you would most likely get a reasonable fill with highly liquid options such as those for MSFT, with index options, if the price is changing and you place a market order, you are likely to get a very unfavorable price. In fact, you could easily fill $5.00 away from your intended price. Using limit orders ensures you will either get the intended price, or your order simply won't fill.

To get a better sense of the liquidity, take a look at the "Volume" column that is shown in the preceding example quotes. Notice the volume is relatively low for all of the options. On this particular day, the highest volume was 512 contracts for the $390 *call* options. Unless they were being used as a hedge, it indicates there was some bullish interest in SOX at the time of these quotes. Though a volume of 512 results in a reasonable amount of liquidity, it is still much lower than a stock such as MSFT, which is typically in the thousands. If the price isn't moving quickly and you placed a market order to buy the $390 *calls*, you might get a fill at the best ask but even if you do, you will already be down about 15 percent on the trade due to the large $2.00 spread ($13.20 − $11.20 = $2.00).

Rather than using a market order and getting filled at the best ask, or even worse, being subject to the whims of the market maker, I generally place a limit order between the best bid and best ask. I'm rarely willing to pay more than a $1.00 premium on the spread just to enter a position. I would rather pass on the trade. Using the $390 *calls* as an example, I might place a limit order at $12.20, or less, depending on how strongly I felt about the trade. I'd prefer to get a fill that is closer to the best bid than the best ask, and since indexes tend to have a much wider range intraday, there's a good chance the price will fluctuate sufficiently to get a fill.

Though I used the $390 *calls* for purposes of discussing liquidity, I actually prefer playing in-the-money index options rather than out-of-the-money options. Even though they cost more and therefore, I'm risking more, I prefer the price action of in-the-money options. So, using the preceding example, I would be more inclined to buy the $355 or $360 *calls* rather than the $390 *calls.*

Also notice that some of the last trades on the previous SOX quote screen are outside of the range of the best bid and ask. In some cases, it could simply be the result of passing time and changing prices since the last trade. In other instances, it could mean that someone received a very poor order fill.

Figure 7.5 is another example that shows December option quotes for the S&P 100 Index (OEX). The index was trading at $475.02 at the time of the quotes.

Since the OEX is more actively traded, notice the correspondingly higher volume and liquidity on the preceding quote screen. Unlike the prior SOX example, you'll see numerous OEX options that have trading volumes numbering in the thousands. As a result, also notice the tighter price spreads between the bids and asks and the higher amounts of open interest.

As explained in the "Options Primer" chapter, open interest reflects the number of option contracts/positions that are currently open, where volume reflects the number of trades both in and out of positions.

Looking at the OEX "Bid/Ask Spread" column, whereas the spreads were frequently $2.00 to $3.00 for the SOX, the OEX spreads that have the highest volume and liquidity are in the range of $0.30 to $0.70.

However, some of the lower-volume spreads are over $1.00, which illustrates the impact that low liquidity can have on the prices.

As usual, you can see that the OEX option premiums decrease the further out of the money the options become. For example, the best ask of the $475 *call* options is $12.10, while the best ask of the $490 *call* options is $5.50. Though the cost of the $490 *calls* is considerably less,

SymID	Root	PutCall	Symbol	ExpDate	syscode	Strike	Last	Bid	Ask	Volume	Theoretical	Imp Volatility	ProvC
63	OEX	C	%OEXF1915900000	Jun 19 2015	296452	900.000	36	32.5	34.6	0			
64	OEX	C	%OEXF1915905000	Jun 19 2015	296234	905.000	31.45	28.1	30.2	0			31.
65	OEX	C	%OEXF1915910000	Jun 19 2015	296229	910.000	20.2	23.9	25.5	0			20
66	OEX	C	%OEXF1915915000	Jun 19 2015	296232	915.000	15.9	19.8	21.4	0			15
67	OEX	C	%OEXF1915920000	Jun 19 2015	296233	920.000	16.2	16	17.4	4			12
68	OEX	C	%OEXF1915925000	Jun 19 2015	296174	925.000	10	12.4	13.7	0			
69	OEX	C	%OEXF1915930000	Jun 19 2015	296080	930.000	10.2	9	10.3	39			9
70	OEX	C	%OEXF1915935000	Jun 19 2015	296143	935.000	8	6.1	7.2	17			6
71	OEX	C	%OEXF1915940000	Jun 19 2015	296135	940.000	4.1	3.8	4.7	52			3
72	OEX	C	%OEXF1915945000	Jun 19 2015	296228	945.000	3.3	2.1	2.85	25			2.
73	OEX	C	%OEXF1915950000	Jun 19 2015	296249	950.000	1.5	0.95	1.5	1			1
74	OEX	C	%OEXF1915955000	Jun 19 2015	296945	955.000	0.55	0.4	0.65	0			0.
75	OEX	C	%OEXF1915960000	Jun 19 2015	296976	960.000	0.25	0.15	0.3	200			0.
76	OEX	C	%OEXF1915965000	Jun 19 2015	297080	965.000	0.15	0.1	0.2	0			0.

Figure 7.5 December Option Quotes for S&P 500 (OEX)

they are over 20 points out of the money ($490 option – $475 index price + $5.50 premium = $20.50). As I discussed earlier, though I trade out-of-the-money options as well, my overall preference is to trade in-the-money options. If I wanted to buy *call* options in this case, I would likely buy the $465 *calls*, or possibly the $470 *calls.*

Trading index options may not be practical for traders with relatively small accounts, especially when you take into consideration that options can't be traded on margin. However, if your account is sufficiently large to make trading index options practical, they can be a great alternative for hedging, or for short-term trades when you anticipate large moves in the market. Since index options tend to move rapidly with large incremental price moves, you can achieve huge gains if you catch a dramatic market move.

I like using index options when I have a strong trend backing up my trade. For example, after a recent FOMC meeting the market gyrated wildly intraday, moving 100+ points in both directions in a matter of minutes. Large, dramatic market moves such as this provide fantastic trading opportunities for index options. Therefore, if I think there is going to be a large market move, rather than hunting for individual stocks, I prefer to be in the indexes.

LEAPs

As a short-term trader, I don't trade LEAPs (Long-Term Equity Anticipation Securities), but for those of you who might be curious about them, I'll provide a general description.

LEAPs are options whose expiration month is nine months or more away. The options quote screen in Figure 7.6 shows a LEAP for QLGC. At the time of these quotes, the option was approximately a year from expiration, and the QLGC stock price was $43.25.

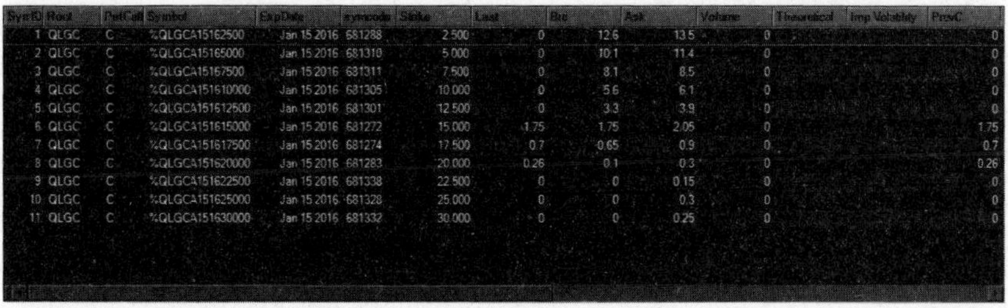

SymID	Root	PutCall	Symbol	ExpDate	symcode	Strike	Last	Bid	Ask	Volume	Theoretical	Imp Volatility	PrevC
1	QLGC	C	%QLGCA15162500	Jan 15 2016	681288	2.500	0	12.6	13.5	0			0
2	QLGC	C	%QLGCA15165000	Jan 15 2016	681310	5.000	0	10.1	11.4	0			0
3	QLGC	C	%QLGCA15167500	Jan 15 2016	681311	7.500	0	8.1	8.5	0			0
4	QLGC	C	%QLGCA151610000	Jan 15 2016	681305	10.000	0	5.6	6.1	0			0
5	QLGC	C	%QLGCA151612500	Jan 15 2016	681301	12.500	0	3.3	3.9	0			0
6	QLGC	C	%QLGCA151615000	Jan 15 2016	681272	15.000	1.75	1.75	2.05	0			1.75
7	QLGC	C	%QLGCA151617500	Jan 15 2016	681274	17.500	0.7	0.65	0.9	0			0.7
8	QLGC	C	%QLGCA151620000	Jan 15 2016	681283	20.000	0.26	0.1	0.3	0			0.26
9	QLGC	C	%QLGCA151622500	Jan 15 2016	681338	22.500	0	0	0.15	0			0
10	QLGC	C	%QLGCA151625000	Jan 15 2016	681328	25.000	0	0	0.3	0			0
11	QLGC	C	%QLGCA151630000	Jan 15 2016	681332	30.000	0	0	0.25	0			0

Figure 7.6 LEAP for QLGC

If you were bullish on QLogic (QLGC) and wanted to speculate long-term that the price would go up, rather than buying the stock, you could consider buying LEAP options. However, as you might expect, you would have to pay a hefty premium for the privilege of such long-term options speculations. In fact, it's questionable whether the premium costs justify using the options over simply buying the stock outright.

Looking at the prior quote screen, you can see that the best ask for the $40 in-the-money *call* is $15.40. Upon expiration, the stock price would need to be $55.40 ($40 + $15.40) or higher to make money on the trade. If you felt there was going to be a large bull run on the stock, you could consider using out-of-the-money options at a lower cost. For example, the best ask for the $50 *call* is quoted as $11.30. Though the initial cost is less in this case, you would need the price to climb to $61.30 ($50 + $11.30) or higher to come out on the trade at options expiration.

It's not likely that I would ever speculate that far out by using LEAPs. Considering my personal objectives and short-term trading style, it really doesn't come up as a consideration for me.

Straddles

One of my favorite options strategies, and one that I use often, is called a straddle. A straddle is buying equal amounts of *calls* and *puts* for the same stock, using the same expiration month, and at the same strike price.

Straddles are a great way to potentially profit from large near-term price moves. In situations where you anticipate a large near-term move but you aren't sure which direction the price will move, you can take advantage of the expected price volatility by using straddles.

Even though I do play them at other times, and for other reasons, I particularly like playing straddles during earnings season when the risk/reward for straddles is quite favorable.

It's common for a stock to move dramatically one way or the other after a company reports earnings, but the direction of the move depends on the specifics of the earnings report, which generally isn't known in advance. If a company blows out earnings estimates, its stock price may be propelled dramatically higher. Conversely, if there is bad news and a company misses earnings estimates or releases an earnings warning, its stock price may plunge. Most stocks will move one direction or the other to some degree after reporting earnings, and an option straddle is a strategy you can use to take advantage of these moves.

Since it is possible, or even probable, that you will lose on one side of a straddle play, you need a sufficiently large move on the other side to make up for the loss and make a profit overall. However, there have been occasions when I've made money on both sides of the trade. For example, a company might initially run higher after blowing out an earnings estimate, which lets you roll out of your *calls*, and then it could sell off later, providing the opportunity to exit your *puts* with a profit as well. Still, this doesn't occur often, so straddles work best when the combined option premiums are sufficiently low to make the trade practical.

I've found the best opportunities occur for stocks that are reporting earnings during the week of option expirations. Option premiums are lower as their expiration dates approach and the earnings reports generate the needed price volatility. In fact, since the goal of traders is to obtain an "edge," or advantage, whenever possible, I've found option expirations week to be one of the best times for trading options. It's one of the few times that you have an edge when trading options because the earnings volatility isn't fully priced into the value of the options.

During earnings season, I typically perform considerably more research, especially just ahead of option expirations week. Not only am I continuing to look for the opportunity to trade stocks long for an earnings run, I'm researching option premiums for potential straddles.

I review earnings calendars and do historical research for the momentum stocks that are scheduled to report earnings during the last week of option expirations. The most promising trading candidates are stocks that have a historical tendency to move dramatically after reporting earnings.

Once I find some stocks that look appealing from a historical perspective, I check the option premiums for those stocks. The combined premium for playing a straddle has to be reasonable, which isn't always the case. I'm not going to pay $6.00 to play a straddle at the money, since I would need a ridiculously large move to make money. However, when the option premiums are attractive and a stock otherwise looks like a good straddle candidate, then I will trade the straddle. For example, I recently traded an EMC straddle with a total cost of about $0.50 and sold it for around $0.70 or so overall. To me, that was a nice risk/reward for a straddle play.

I've made a considerable amount of money trading option straddles over the years, as have many of my clients, especially when the market traded at the lofty levels that it did in the late 1990s. I recall making about $26.00 per contract, or about $140,000 total, on an overnight PMCS straddle. We've also had numerous other great straddle trades. Of course, not all trades are profitable, nor do they all net such nice gains, but it's still not uncommon to achieve 15 percent or 20 percent gains overall, or $5.00 to $10.00 moves, and even an occasional double or better can occur when a trade goes particularly well. Regardless of the specific amount, whenever it's a gain rather than a loss, I'm happy to take whatever the market gives me!

Though the majority of my straddle trades take place during earnings season and the last week of option expirations, whenever attractive premiums and sufficient volatility allow, I will trade straddles at other times.

For example, I've used straddles to trade FOMC meetings. Since the market is often volatile when the results of FOMC meetings are announced, you can sometimes trade it using a straddle and profit from a move in both directions. Essentially, anytime there is the potential for a lot of volatility in the market, it could be a good opportunity to use a straddle. In a best-case scenario, a volatile up-and-down market could let you roll out of both your *calls* and *puts* with a profit.

Figure 7.7 is an options quote screen for eBay in which the stock price is $70.10.

I prefer straddles where the option strike prices are very near or *at the money*. Meaning, the strike price for both options is as close

SymID	Root	PutCall	Symbol	ExpDate	Eproode	Strike	Last	Bid	Ask	Volume	Theoretical	Imp Volatility	PremC
29	EBAY	C	%EBAYF191558000	Jun 19 2015	100987	58.000	4.93	3.6	4.1	0			4
30	EBAY	C	%EBAYF191558500	Jun 19 2015	100969	58.500	3.6	3.45	3.65	12			4
31	EBAY	C	%EBAYF191559000	Jun 19 2015	100949	59.000	3	3	3.2	8			3
32	EBAY	C	%EBAYF191559500	Jun 19 2015	100933	59.500	2.52	2.57	2.71	4			2
33	EBAY	C	%EBAYF191560000	Jun 19 2015	100896	60.000	2.3	2.24	2.3	43			2
34	EBAY	C	%EBAYF191560500	Jun 19 2015	100899	60.500	1.8	1.86	1.92	2			2
35	EBAY	C	%EBAYF191561000	Jun 19 2015	100895	61.000	1.52	1.52	1.58	90			1
36	EBAY	C	%EBAYF191561500	Jun 19 2015	100897	61.500	1.22	1.21	1.27	37			
37	EBAY	C	%EBAYF191562000	Jun 19 2015	100900	62.000	0.96	0.97	1.01	60			1
38	EBAY	C	%EBAYF191562500	Jun 19 2015	100902	62.500	0.8	0.75	0.79	54			0
39	EBAY	C	%EBAYF191563000	Jun 19 2015	100919	63.000	0.56	0.58	0.61	61			

Figure 7.7   December Options Quote for EBAY

as possible to the stock's price. This lets you pay roughly an equal amount for both the *calls* and *puts.*

Looking at the preceding quote screen, notice that the EBAY stock price is $70.10 and the $70 *call* and *put* options are closely priced at $2.85 and $2.75, respectively. To play a straddle, you would buy an equal amount of the $70 *calls* and the $70 *puts* for a total combined cost of $5.60 for the straddle ($2.85 + $2.75 = $5.60).

Note that I'm simply using this quote screen for illustration purposes only. In my opinion, the premiums in this case are actually still too high, since the options were more than a week away from expiration at the time of the quotes. During the final week of option expirations, the premiums would be somewhere in the range of $1.20 or so, which would make them reasonable to consider for a straddle. The total cost of the straddle would be around $2.40, so EBAY would only need to move about 5 percent to make money on the trade, and it is fairly common for momentum stocks such as EBAY to move by 5 percent or more following an earnings report.

Even though there is risk associated with playing straddles, you generally don't lose an unreasonable amount. You can typically roll out of the trade on one side or the other with at least most of your original investment, or more. Still, if EBAY were to open essentially flat, you would lose on both sides of the trade due to the short time frame until the options expire, and the resulting loss of the time-based portion of the option premiums. You might even lose half of your money in such a scenario. Fortunately, this rarely occurs with volatile momentum stocks such as EBAY. Volatile stocks tend to move up and down sufficiently to let you roll out of your positions. Still, the potential for loss is a reality that you should take into account before making the decision to speculate using a straddle.

Ideally, as mentioned earlier, unless you intentionally have a bullish or bearish bias, you should use *call* and *put* options for a straddle whose strike prices are as close as possible to the stock's price so that the premiums for each position are reasonably close in price as well. Otherwise, your straddle will have an inherent bullish or bearish bias.

For example, if the preceding EBAY stock price were $69 rather than $70.10, you would have a bias toward the short side since the $70 *puts* would already be in the money, and would be more expensive than the $70 *calls.*

Strangles

Strangles are similar to straddles, except you use out-of-the-money strike prices that are different from one another. A strangle is buying equal amounts of *calls* and *puts* for the same stock, using the same expiration month, at two different out-of-the-money strike prices that surround the stock's price.

For illustration purposes, I'll use the EBAY quote screen that was shown earlier (see Figure 7.8).

Looking at the preceding quotes, if you wanted to buy an EBAY strangle, you could buy the $65 *put* and $75 *call* options. You are splitting the difference between the stock price and the option strike prices. In this case, the $65 *put* is roughly $5.00 less than the $70.10 stock price, and the $75 *call* is roughly $5.00 greater than the stock price. By playing a strangle, you are betting that the stock will either go lower than $65.00 or higher than $75.00.

The combined cost of the strangle would be $2.05 ($1.15 + $0.90).

As before, these quotes are just for illustration purposes and are more than a week out away from the option expiration date. The actual combined cost would be about $1.00, if you waited until the final week of option expirations, which is the approach that I generally use.

Since you are further out of the money when trading a strangle, you typically need the stock's price to move farther in order to come out on the trade. Rather than about a 5 percent move, as described earlier for the EBAY straddle, you now need EBAY to move around 10 percent. In order to cover the hypothetical $1.00 option premium and the desired $5.00 price move, the stock's price needs to move more than $6.00 (i.e., about 10%) in either direction prior to option expirations. Even so, a 10 percent move is quite possible for a volatile

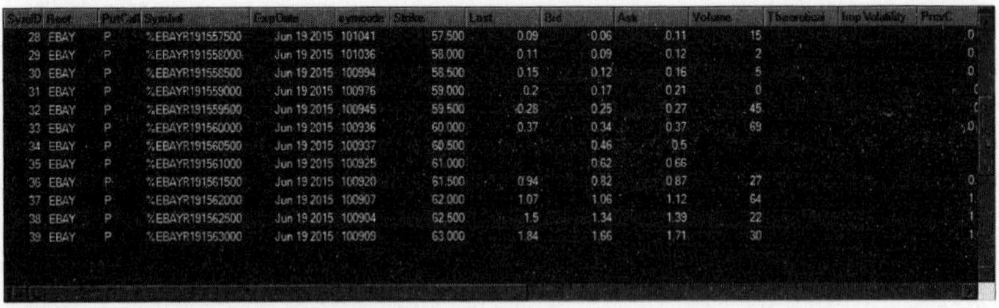

Symbol	Root	Put/Call	Symbol	ExpDate	symcode	Strike	Last	Bid	Ask	Volume	Theoretical	Imp Volatility	ProxC
28	EBAY	P	.EBAYR191557500	Jun 19 2015	101041	57.500	0.09	0.06	0.11	15			0
29	EBAY	P	.EBAYR191558000	Jun 19 2015	101036	58.000	0.11	0.09	0.12	2			0
30	EBAY	P	.EBAYR191558500	Jun 19 2015	100894	58.500	0.15	0.12	0.16	5			0
31	EBAY	P	.EBAYR191559000	Jun 19 2015	100976	59.000	0.2	0.17	0.21	0			0
32	EBAY	P	.EBAYR191559500	Jun 19 2015	100945	59.500	0.28	0.25	0.27	45			0
33	EBAY	P	.EBAYR191560000	Jun 19 2015	100936	60.000	0.37	0.34	0.37	69			0
34	EBAY	P	.EBAYR191560500	Jun 19 2015	100937	60.500		0.46	0.5				
35	EBAY	P	.EBAYR191561000	Jun 19 2015	100925	61.000		0.62	0.66				
36	EBAY	P	.EBAYR191561500	Jun 19 2015	100920	61.500	0.94	0.82	0.87	27			0
37	EBAY	P	.EBAYR191562000	Jun 19 2015	100907	62.000	1.07	1.06	1.12	64			1
38	EBAY	P	.EBAYR191562500	Jun 19 2015	100904	62.500	1.5	1.34	1.39	22			1
39	EBAY	P	.EBAYR191563000	Jun 19 2015	100909	63.000	1.84	1.65	1.71	30			1

Figure 7.8   EBAY Quote Screen

momentum stock such as EBAY, so it's not unreasonable to consider using a strangle when the option premiums and other circumstances of a trade indicate the risk/reward remains favorable overall.

As I mentioned earlier, although I've made a lot of money trading these option plays, keep in mind that they are speculative in nature. Therefore, you should only use a small portion of your total funds for such speculative trades.

Bull Spread

A *bull spread* is a bullish option strategy you can use when you think a stock's price is more likely to go higher than it is to go lower.

To trade a bull spread, you buy *call* options for a stock, and sell an equal amount of *call* options for the same stock at a price that is a strike price, or a few strike prices, higher.

The *call* option you buy is typically in the money, or closer to the money, than the *call* option you sell. You pay the premium for the option you buy, and collect the premium for the option you sell. The end result is that the overall bias for a bull spread is as its name implies, bullish.

A bull spread lowers your risk for the trade to the amount you paid for the option you bought, less the premium you collected from the option you sold. The maximum reward is limited, however, since it falls between the two strike prices. Although the profits are limited, the risk is much lower as well.

I will sometimes trade a bull spread during earnings season when I think there is a greater chance than not that a stock will move higher ahead of its earnings report.

Figure 7.9 is a sample options quote screen for KLAC. At the time of these quotes, KLAC was scheduled to report earnings in about two weeks. The KLAC stock price was $42.85 at the time of the quotes.

Figure 7.9   Options Quote Screen for KLAC

Knowing that KLAC is reporting earnings in two weeks and that it historically runs up ahead of its earnings report, you might consider playing the anticipated bullish bias using a bull spread. Referring to the preceding quote screen, there are a number of ways you could play the bull spread.

One approach is to buy the $40 *in-the-money calls* at $4.50 and sell *out-of-the-money* $45 *calls* at $1.75. Since you are selling the $45 *calls*, you would collect the $1.75 premium, then pay the $4.50 premium on the $40 *calls* you are buying, so your net out-of-pocket cost for the bull spread would be $2.75 ($4.50 – $1.75). The in-the-money *calls* and higher cost on the buy side reflect your bullish bias.

If KLAC is $45.00 or higher by options expiration, you would make a maximum of $2.25 on the trade, which is the difference between the $45 options you sold and the $40 options you bought, less the net cost of the options (e.g., $45.00 – $40.00 – $2.75 = $2.25).

Alternatively, for further clarification the value of each option could be determined. If the KLAC stock price was $45.00, you would be up $5.00 on the $40 *calls* you bought. Since the option premium was $4.50, you would make $0.50 on the trade ($5.00 – $4.50 = $0.50). The value of the $45 *calls* you sold would be zero, but you would collect the $1.75 premium. The end result is the same. You would make $2.25 on the bull spread ($0.50 + $1.75 = $2.25).

If the KLAC stock price is $40 or less at expiration, the most you can lose on the trade is the net premium cost of the options, which is $2.75. You would gain or lose a proportionate amount when the KLAC stock price is in between the two strike prices. Meaning, you would lose an amount between zero and the maximum of $2.75, or gain an amount between zero and the maximum of $2.25, if the stock's price remains between the two strike prices of the options.

If you were particularly bullish on the stock, you could consider using options that are further out of the money. Your potential profits would be greater, but the stock would need to move further to fully realize all of the profits.

For example, looking at the preceding illustration again, you could buy the $45 *calls* at $1.75 and sell the $50 *calls* at $0.50, which results in a net cost of $1.25. In this scenario, you would need an earnings run to propel the price to $50 or higher to realize the maximum potential profit of $3.75 ($50 – $45 – $1.25 = $3.75). The stock has to run further, but if it does, you could potentially net 200% on your money. The most you could lose is the $1.25 net cost.

With bull spreads, if the price continues to move further above the strike price of the *calls* you sell, you would still net only the maximum potential profit. In the preceding example, if the price ran to $60 or higher, your maximum profit would still be $3.75.

While you would make more on the $45 *calls* you bought, you would give back the same amount in additional losses on the $50 *calls* you sold.

Determining precisely when and how to exit a bull spread is dependent on the specifics of the trade and your own preferences. As explained earlier, you need not wait for the options to expire to exit a trade. You can take profits whenever you are satisfied with your gains, or you can exit a position simply to limit losses.

However, you generally shouldn't exit the *calls* you bought without also exiting the *calls* you sold, since doing so could leave you exposed to greater risk should the stock's price unexpectedly surge higher (this would be the equivalent of selling the *calls naked*). Without holding the buy position to cover potential losses on the sell position, you could incur significantly higher losses.

Bear Spread

Similar to the way you use a bull spread for an upside bias, you can use a bear spread when your bias is to the downside. A bear spread is essentially the opposite, or reverse, of the previously discussed bull spread.

To trade a bear spread, you buy *put* options for a stock, and sell an equal amount of *put* options for the same stock at a price that is a strike price, or a few strike prices, lower.

The *put* option you buy is in the money, or closer to the money, than the *put* option you sell. As before, you pay the premium for the option you buy, and collect the premium for the option you sell. The end result is that the overall bias for a bear spread is bearish.

As with a bull spread, a bear spread lowers your risk for the trade to the amount you pay for the option you buy, less the premium you collect from the option you sell. The maximum reward is limited, however, since it falls between the two strike prices. And although the profits are limited, the risk is lower as well.

Figure 7.10 is a sample options quote screen for EXPE. The EXPE stock price is $75.08.

SymID Root	PutCall	Symbol	ExpDate	symcode	Strike	Last	Bid	Ask	Volume	Theoretical	Imp Volatility	PorvC
28 EXPE	P	%EXPER191510000	Jun 19 2015	245583	100.000	0.41	0.6	0.75	0			0.
29 EXPE	P	%EXPER191510100	Jun 19 2015	245571	101.000	0.56	0.8	0.9	0			0.
30 EXPE	P	%EXPER191510200	Jun 19 2015	245500	102.000	1.1	1.05	1.15	6			0
31 EXPE	P	%EXPER191510300	Jun 19 2015	245466	103.000	1.25	1.3	1.45	4			0.
32 EXPE	P	%EXPER191510400	Jun 19 2015	245462	104.000	1.15	1.65	1.8	0			1.
33 EXPE	P	%EXPER191510500	Jun 19 2015	245437	105.000	2.05	2.05	2.25	6			1
34 EXPE	P	%EXPER191510600	Jun 19 2015	245433	106.000	2.05	2.55	2.8	0			2
35 EXPE	P	%EXPER191510700	Jun 19 2015	245426	107.000	2.25	3.1	3.4	0			2.
36 EXPE	P	%EXPER191510800	Jun 19 2015	245429	108.000	1.9	3.7	4	0			1
37 EXPE	P	%EXPER191510900	Jun 19 2015	245435	109.000	3.19	4.4	4.8	0			3.
38 EXPE	P	%EXPER191511000	Jun 19 2015	245442	110.000	5.05	5.2	5.5	6			4
39 EXPE	P	%EXPER191511100	Jun 19 2015	245447	111.000	5.3	6	6.4	0			5

Figure 7.10   Options Quote Screen for EXPE

Similar to the bull spread, you can choose among a number of strategies to play a bear spread. For example, you could buy the $75 *puts* at $4.20 and sell the $70 *puts* at $2.40. Your net cost for the trade would be $1.80, which is the premium you paid for the $75 *puts* minus the premium you collected for the $70 *puts* that you sold ($4.20 – $2.40 = $1.80). If the price of EXPE moves to $70 or lower, you make $3.20 on the trade ($75 – $70 – $1.80).

Alternatively, if you wanted to go further out of the money on the trade, you could consider buying the $75 *puts* at $4.20, and rather than selling the $70 *puts*, you could sell the $65 *puts* at $1.30. The net cost in this case would be $2.90. If the price of EXPE moves to $65.00 or lower, you would make $7.10 on the trade ($75 – $65 – $2.90).

Though the potential profits are higher when you go further out of the money, the stock price has to move further as well. My preference would be the $75/$70 spread in this case, since the associated cost and risk is less.

As with the bull spread, you need not wait for the options to expire to exit a bear spread. You can take profits anytime you choose, or you can exit a losing position to help reduce the maximum potential losses.

And once again, you generally shouldn't exit the *puts* you bought without also exiting the *puts* you sold, since doing so could leave you exposed to greater risk should the stock's price fall unexpectedly (in this case, it would be the equivalent of selling the *puts naked*). Without holding the *buy* position to cover potential losses on the *sell* position, you could incur significantly higher losses.

Trading Gaps Animal Spirit Guide (Stalking, Leopard)

This chapter provides more detailed gap-related information than I've provided thus far. It explains what gaps are, what causes gaps, when gaps occur, and more. Suggestions and examples for trading both gap ups and gap downs are included. Chapter 10, "Trading Gaps Using Technical Analysis," supplements the information presented here with additional techniques for trading gaps that are based primarily on charts and technical analysis. You'll find charting techniques there to determine specific price targets for entering and exiting gap trades. As previously discussed, trading morning gaps is a great way to trade the market on a part-time basis. If you desire to trade part-time and can spare an hour or so in the mornings when the market first opens for trading, then I suggest you give trading gaps a try. And for full-time traders, gaps often provide some of the best trading opportunities of the day. I know many traders who merely trade the gap and "go home," having made their daily goals in an hour or less most days. Hence, this is why gap trading is often referred to by *moi* as "The One-Hour Trader." In fact, we offer a specific service at Affinity Trading just to trade the gaps!

What Are Gaps?

There are essentially three ways that the price of a stock can open for trading relative to its prior closing price. It can open higher, lower, or at the same price. When there is a difference between a stock's closing price and its opening price, it is called a *gap*. If the opening price is higher than the prior closing price, it's called a gap up. If the price is lower, it's a gap down. When a stock opens at essentially the same price as the prior close, or the difference is very small, then it's considered to be a flat open. Table 8.1 shows some price examples of gaps (examples are provided in Figure 8.1).

You can see from the INTC chart in Figure 8.1 that one of the cool things about gaps is that the same stock can be played every way. The same stock will gap *up* at times, open *flat* at times, and gap *down* sometimes.

A stock that has a reasonable degree of liquidity rarely opens at exactly the same price as its prior close. Whether it is large, medium, or small, a stock generally gaps by some amount. However, if the price difference is so small that it is essentially a flat open, you generally shouldn't try to trade the open as a gap play since a price reversal is less certain. Gaps not only apply to individual stocks, they apply to the overall market as well. Since the market is a collection of individual stocks, if the market is gapping up or down significantly, then a large number of individual stocks are likely gapping up or down as well. Figure 8.2 shows a gap down of the Nasdaq Composite.

For the moment, just notice on the chart that the Nasdaq Composite opened considerably lower, or gapped down, from where it closed the prior day, which means that a large number of technology stocks within the Nasdaq likely gapped down as well. What causes gaps? A variety of factors can cause the market or individual stocks to gap. Examples include late-breaking news on specific stocks, earnings reports, analyst upgrades or downgrades, overnight futures trading, economic news, major world events, or simply an imbalance between supply and demand. Regardless of the specific catalyst, gaps occur due to excess demand on the buy or sell side, which is further exaggerated by low-volume trading that takes place outside of regular market hours. Since the total number of buyers and sellers is lower during post- and pre-market hours, any significant buying pressure pushes stock prices higher than would normally

Table 8.1   Stock Close/Open Difference

Close 52.25 Open $52.75 Gap UP .50 cents
Close $14.72 Open $14.50 Gap DOWN .22 cents
Close $27.93 Open $27.93 FLAT—NO GAP!

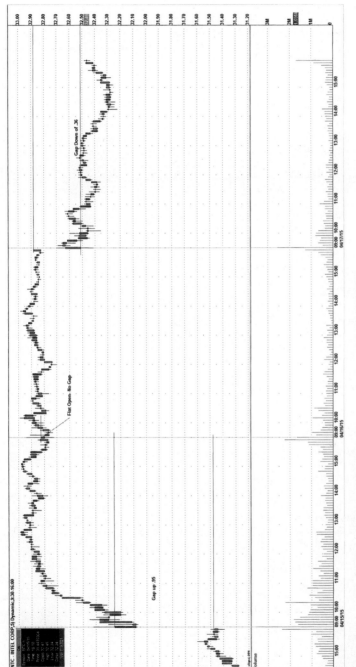

Figure 8.1 INTC $.95 cent Gap UP; Flat Open: .36 cent Gap DOWN

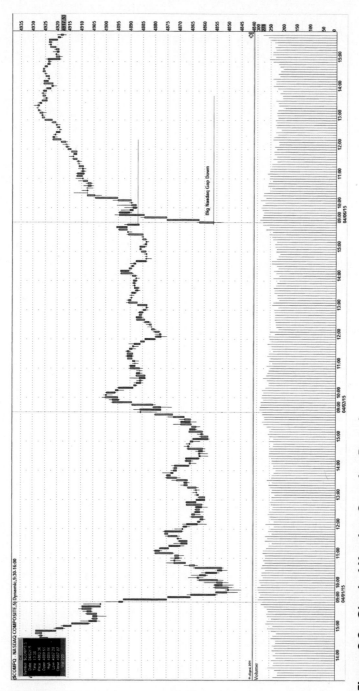

Figure 8.2   Chart of Nasdaq Gapping Down!

occur during regular market hours. The opposite is true when there is more selling pressure. Emotions play a role as well. Large gaps often result from traders overreacting to news in after-hours trading. Not wanting to miss out on a big move, people get excited and buy or sell impulsively, causing the prices to move even more dramatically. Once the market opens and liquidity returns to normal, the exaggerated prices tend to correct themselves with a snapback price reversal.

For example, take a look at what happened on the prior chart of the Nasdaq Composite. After the large gap down, there was initially a snapback price reversal to the upside. Understanding this, agile power traders can potentially profit by anticipating and trading these snapback price reversals. This is also called fading the gap. As the buying or selling pressure that caused the gap subsides, prices tend to fade in the opposite direction. Filling the gap is when a stock, or the market, ends up retracing the entire gap at some point. A stock that closed at $25.50 and gapped up to $26.10 only to retrace the move back to $25.50 has filled the gap. Many technical analysts will tell you they believe that almost all stocks (and the market itself) will invariably fill their gaps. I don't necessarily agree with this statement, as I've seen too many gaps over the years *not* filled. However, it's worth noting that many, if not most, *intraday* gaps do fill. Those are the ones we are keying on here, so it's an important statement.

When do gaps occur? Although the size of gaps varies, they occur almost every single market day. On a given day, gaps are generally traded during the first 30 minutes of the day. The short time frame for trading gaps is why they provide such a great part-time trading opportunity. The length of a gap trade can range from seconds to minutes, to hours, or occasionally, all day if a gap reversal gains momentum in the opposite direction and you decide to trail the move for as long as possible. On a weekly basis, it's been my experience that the best days for gaps tend to be Mondays and Fridays, though any day of the week could turn out to be a good day. Increased uncertainty is one of the reasons. Going into a new week, no one knows for certain how the market will behave, either that day or for the rest of the week. Similarly, the uncertainty going into the weekend is a factor on Fridays, though less so than for Mondays. The increased uncertainty often causes more volatility, which results in larger gaps. Although there are occasions when a stock is halted during the day due to pending news or for reasons other than gaps when it reopens for trading, it's the morning gaps that we are interested in as traders because they provide the most predictable and consistent trading opportunities.

Planning Your Gap Trade

Even though gap plays are generally quick, short-term trades, a reasonable amount of preparation is still needed in order to achieve the best results. Obviously, you'll need to determine which stocks are gapping and which of those may offer the best trading opportunities. Additionally, to properly prepare you should review the overall news and market conditions, news pertaining to individual stocks of interest, pre-market activity and price action, volume and order flow, what type of setups to use for potential trade entries, how to best manage risk and take profits, what lot size to use on a given trade, and so on. Following are some general tips and techniques that I use when trading gaps. In Chapter 10, I'll discuss a variety of other techniques you can use to help plan entry and exit strategies that are based upon charts and technical analysis. Since there are a variety of tools and techniques from which to choose, I suggest that you read both chapters about trading gaps and try out the approaches that seem to work best for you. If one doesn't work out well, you can try another. As is often the case, techniques that work well for one person may not work as well for someone else, so after some experimentation and as you gain more experience, you'll be in a better position to determine which techniques best suit your personal goals and trading style. If you do decide to use the technical analysis techniques that are discussed in the next chapter, I highly recommend that you still take into account the information provided in this chapter when planning your trades. The information provided in the next chapter is intended to supplement the information presented here.

Daily Gap Goals!

Many traders set daily profit goals. Whether or not to do so is really a matter of personal choice, but I personally believe it's beneficial not only to have trading goals, but to have general life-oriented goals as well. After all, before you can realize your dreams you need to know what they are. I suggest that you create a written list. Then, you can define the series of steps needed to accomplish each item on your list by breaking them down into smaller, more easily achieved goals.

Before you know it, many of your seemingly out-of-reach dreams may become your new reality. Of course, your goals should be reasonable and realistic, but that doesn't mean that they can't be far reaching, even to the point of becoming a multimillionaire! While you might not be able to achieve such lofty goals overnight, you very well could at some point in the future. I'm including a discussion of this topic here because if you do set a daily profit goal, the exit strategy for your gap trades could be affected. For example, if your daily profit goal is $300, you'll need to decide what you will do if you are still holding positions when you hit your daily goal. On a good day, you could potentially hit such a daily goal with a single gap trade. If you bought 1000 shares of XYZ stock on a large gap down and it moved by $0.30 in your favor, you would hit your daily goal. If that happens, what will you do? Will you immediately close out all of your positions and quit for the day, or will you continue trading? Many traders consider their job done once they hit their daily goal. Not wanting to risk giving back any of their hard-earned profits, they immediately close out positions, quit, and enjoy the rest of the day off. Other traders go for all they can get and continue trading after meeting their daily goal. And yet others may use the remaining time for learning or experimenting. You can use the time to try out new tactics by paper trading or trading in demo mode rather than risking your real capital. If you discover new techniques that work well, they can be incorporated into your trading strategies. Once again, this is really a matter of personal preference and what works best for you. If you find that you tend to make a good profit in the mornings and end up giving it back later in the day, then it might be best to quit once your daily goal has been met. As discussed in the "Intraday Time Frames" chapter, there are frequently lulls in the market at certain times of the day. Attempting to trade these could result in a churning of your account with little or no gains, or even worse, losses.

If you intend to set a daily profit goal, you must first determine what amount is reasonable and realistic, taking into consideration the size of your trading account. Obviously, it's not realistic to expect to make 50 percent on your account each day. And, the amount that is reasonable for a $5,000 account won't be the same as for a $10,000 account, a $50,000 account, a $5,000,000 account, and so on. While the specific amount is subjective and in part dependent on your level of experience, the size of your account, as well as other factors, generally, I feel a daily goal that is about 2 percent of your account size is realistic, especially once you've mastered trend-trading techniques. Therefore, if you have a $10,000 account, your daily goal based on 2 percent would be $200.

Of course, you are not likely to achieve your daily goal every day. Some days, and possibly even some weeks or months, you will lose money. But hopefully, and in order to be successful over the long-term, you will have more winning days overall than losing days, and the upside potential of having a daily goal of just 2 percent can be quite large on average over a period of time. As the size of your account increases, the size of your daily goal will increase.

Objectives

Your expectations and objectives for a trade can influence both how you manage the trade, and how you exit it. If you have realistic expectations and objectives going into a trade, you will be less likely to make impulsive decisions that are based on emotion rather than a predetermined plan. You'll also be in a better position to plan entry and exit strategies, manage your risk, and consider strategies for taking profits. With that in mind, what are some realistic expectations for gap trades? Well, you should anticipate any of the following. A gap trade can be fast and volatile, so you may need to react quickly to rapidly changing conditions. A gap trade can be short and easy, or it can last well into the morning, and in some cases, it can even last all day. This, at least in many instances, depends on your objectives for the trade, how you manage it, and how much time you have available to devote to trading on a given day.

Gaps create opportunities to achieve nice profits in short time frames, but it's also possible to lose money in short time frames. The objectives you set for a trade will likely affect the outcome of the trade as well. Do you plan to take profits and quit once your daily profit goals have been met, even if there could potentially be additional gains left in a trade? Are you prepared to trade throughout the morning? All day? Or, do you need to quit trading within the first hour, and perhaps go to another job? Do you have predetermined price targets, or do you plan to simply play it for what you can get? Of course, another obvious objective is to make a profit, but what if the trade goes against you? Since that's a possibility, another objective should be to predefine and limit losses as well. These are only a few examples of how your expectations and objectives could potentially affect the outcome of a trade but as you can see, if you think about them in advance, you'll at least be in a better position to factor them into your trading plan. More specific ways of doing this are provided later in this chapter, and in the next chapter.

News/News/News

The news can play an important role in planning and tracking your trades. Before the market opens each morning, I look for momentum stocks that are gapping up or down without a good reason, meaning on no substantial news. The larger the gap, the better the potential trade. Since the preference is to find stocks that are gapping without a good reason, you should always review the news before planning your gap trades, and then keep an eye on the news while executing your trades as well. Initially, you'll want to determine whether stocks are gapping for a good reason based on substantial news, or whether the gaps are overly exaggerated on no news, and as a result are more likely to reverse direction. You should take into account any news that could affect the market at large, and news related to the individual stocks you choose, including any news related to their sectors or other stocks within their sectors. If there is some type of major news propelling the market one way or the other, you may want to wait a little longer for confirmation of a gap reversal before entering a trade. If an individual stock is gapping up on news such as a major analyst upgrade or an upside earnings announcement, then it is a riskier play. Why would you risk selling it short? It has positive news that could propel the price even higher, or that could keep the price propped up, making a pullback less certain. Instead, you can generally achieve better results by looking for a stock that is gapping up large on no news—preferably, a weak stock in a weak sector that appears overbought. Conversely, when entering a long position on a gap down, it's usually best to look for strong stocks and avoid stocks that have bad news associated with them, or with their sectors. Some of the best opportunities occur when stocks in one sector gap on major news that doesn't apply to stocks in other sectors, but the unrelated stocks gap as well. Stocks that gap for no reason or on news that doesn't pertain to them are good candidates for potential gap reversals.

Interpreting the news, and the reason for gaps, can be subjective and dependent on a large variety of factors, so you should take all of the circumstances into consideration and use your own judgment, preferably with a historical perspective about what has occurred previously under similar conditions. Dramatic gaps will frequently reverse even when they were triggered by a substantial news event, particularly when gaps push stocks further into an oversold or overbought condition. With time and experience, you'll get better at judging which set of conditions provide the best trading opportunities (a touch of instinct about market behavior doesn't hurt, either).

Come Out, Come Out, Wherever You Are, Mr. Gap!

As is often the case, there are a variety of methods and tools you could potentially use to ferret out stocks that are gapping. One approach is to use your broker or quote provider. Some services have features that show which stocks are moving the most in premarket activity. For example, you can try checking the largest percentage gainers and losers, and which stocks are the most active. You can also check the broader markets such as the Nasdaq 100 Stock Index Futures, and the S&P 500 Stock Index Futures. For example, if the Nasdaq is gapping down but the S&P 500 is up slightly, then I would narrow the field by looking for technology stocks that are gapping down. And, as just discussed in the preceding section, the news can also be a good source for gap-trading ideas. Often, stocks that are gapping based on substantial good or bad news impact other stocks in the same business or sector, so you can check the news for potential trading opportunities.

Typically, I look for popular momentum stocks since they tend to gap more dramatically and provide the best opportunity for a corrective price reversal. However, depending on the circumstances, I do play other stocks as well, such as S&P 500 stocks. The idea is to find stocks that will provide the most "bang for the buck." I would rather play a $1.50 EBAY gap down than a $0.30 Citicorp gap down. Since the EBAY gap is considerably larger, the potential price movement on the trade is likely to be considerably larger as well, and the larger the price movement, the greater the potential for a nice profit. Another advantage to using momentum stocks is that they provide greater liquidity and price action, which makes it easier to get in and out of a trade fast (an important consideration for traders). Though not always, momentum stocks generally consist of technology or biotechnology (biotech) stocks that trade on the Nasdaq stock exchange. As a result, they usually have four letters in their symbols such as LinkedIn (LNKD), Cisco (CSCO), and Amgen (AMGN). Note that

I'm only using these particular symbols to illustrate Nasdaq ticker symbols. I'm not suggesting that you use these specific stocks to trade gaps. There are many potential momentum stocks to consider. Which stocks are best varies on a day-to-day basis and is subject to overall market conditions and the specific circumstances of a given trade. Also, I do trade stocks from other exchanges at times. Once I've picked some good trading candidates, I add them to my watch list and start looking for potential trade setups.

Order Flow

As I previously mentioned, the time frame for trading gaps is frequently short, and as a result, the price action can be fast and volatile. Although a gap trade may last for minutes, hours, or even all day, it can also be over in a matter of seconds. In some instances, the action can be so fast that even fractions of a second in order execution speeds can affect the outcome of a trade. For that reason, you really need a fast-order execution system and a Level II quote display. In my opinion, you need a direct-access brokerage account to trade gaps. You can check www.AffinityTrading.com for our current recommendations.

On the whole, web-based brokers simply don't have the consistent, reliable execution speeds you need to get in and out of gap trades quickly enough, even those brokers that advertise fast, 10-second execution speeds. Waiting 10 seconds for an order to execute can be an eternity when trading gaps, and can turn a winning trade into a losing trade. Although any system is subject to occasional technical problems or unanticipated demand loads, generally, order executions are virtually instantaneous (fractions of a second) when using a good direct-access broker with high-speed Internet access.

Once you are set up with a good broker, you'll want to pull up your Level II quote screen and watch the price action and order flow for any stocks of interest. On my Level II quote screen, I pay attention to who is buying or selling my chosen stocks and judge when to get in based on the overall buying or selling pressure. I wait for signs that the buying (for gap ups) or selling (for gap downs) is beginning to subside. To help determine this, I watch the overall size, volume, and quantity of orders on each side for signs that the order flow is stabilizing, or beginning to dry up on the buy side for gap ups, or the sell side for gap downs. If this doesn't occur as expected or as desired for a particular stock, then I look for a different play and don't force the trade. I don't want to take on additional risk by going against particularly heavy buying or selling on the opposite side of my trade. If I'm shorting, however, I may act sooner than when I'm buying long, particularly if the gap is large and appears to be very exaggerated. Since you should try to short into strength, you might end up chasing shares to short if you wait too long (particularly after the selling begins from a snapback price reversal). That's why I prefer gap downs. They are typically easier to play. You can wait longer for confirmation of a reversal and still get in on the move. Still, since the risk/reward for the trade is so favorable, you may not want to wait too long on large gap downs, either.

Managing Risk

Managing risk is a key element to succeeding as a trader, so much so that in addition to this specific discussion, I will frequently include reminders and suggestions for limiting risk throughout the book, most often by suggesting the diligent use of stop-loss orders. In a sense, managing risk is also having a preplanned exit strategy for your trade. It is a preplanned exit strategy for what happens when a trade goes against you. Similarly, taking profits could be thought of as a preplanned exit strategy for what happens when a trade moves in your favor. One of the benefits of playing gaps is that they have unlimited upside potential with limited downside risk *if* you use the proper risk parameters. The downside risk is limited because you can predefine and limit the amount of risk you are willing to accept with the disciplined use of stop-loss orders. And when the price moves in your favor, you can adjust your stop-loss order, or use a trailing stop-loss order and let it run, taking profits along the way according to your plan for the trade. A good approach is to sell a percentage of your shares when your initial profit target is reached, then move your trailing stop-loss order to at least break even on your remaining shares. This ensures that you can't lose on the trade. If an upside move continues, you'll capture additional gains on your remaining shares until the price reverses and you are stopped out of the trade. I'll discuss this more and provide an example in the next section.

Although gaps are high-percentage trends, it always pays to use due diligence and a reasonable degree of caution. Like everything else about the stock market, there are no guarantees. There are days where the market gaps up large, or gaps down large, then just keeps on going the same direction and never looks back. This is when you should use the 10:00 a.m. rule as a guideline. How to trade days like this is discussed in more detail in the next chapter. Other days, although there is almost always some type of a gap, the gap may be modest, making the play more risky. Similarly, if a gap is quite small, the market is considered to be essentially flat from the prior day, in which case it's advisable to wait until the market reveals a direction and not play the gap at all. On the other hand, large gaps are such high percentage plays that, when uncertain, I will often just go ahead and play the gap. If a stock has gapped down large on no news, the risk of it going down considerably further in such a short period of time is relatively low. Since gaps are usually very short-term intraday plays, the risk/reward is even more in your favor, because shorter time frames decrease the time-based risk. Though the price could go down further after a large gap down, if you employ good risk management and use stop-loss orders, your downside risk will be defined and limited. To determine a maximum risk limit, I recommend using the 2 percent rule as a guideline. Meaning, you shouldn't let any single trade go against you by more than 2 percent of the total value of your account. Using the 2 percent rule, if you had a $10,000 account, you shouldn't lose more than $200 on any single trade. Of course, that doesn't mean that you should base all of your stop-loss settings solely on your maximum risk limit. It's intended to be the most you will lose on any given trade.

You should still take into consideration the specific circumstances of each trade. For example, with a $200 maximum risk limit, if you bought 200 shares, you couldn't let the trade go against you by more than $1.00 ($1 × 200 shares = $200 maximum limit). Depending on the price range of a given stock, a $1.00 stop-loss setting might be too much, or too little. Here's another example. Suppose you bought 1,000 shares. Now, your stop-loss setting would need to be $0.20 to remain within your $200 maximum limit ($0.20 × 1,000 = $200). When trading gaps, you would likely get stopped out of most trades with such a small stop-loss setting. Therefore, on any given trade, you need to adjust your lot size such that you can use a reasonable stop-loss cushion and still remain within your maximum risk limit for the trade. I'll discuss using stop-loss orders from a technical analysis perspective in the next chapter.

In general, if you are playing a gap down without using technical analysis, after entering a position you should place an initial stop-loss order slightly beneath the stock's low for the day. Conversely, if you are playing a gap up, place a stop-loss order slightly above the stock's high for the day. Of course, if setting a stop-loss at these points exceeds your maximum risk limit, then you should make appropriate adjustments to either your stop-loss setting or your lot size. Since gap trades tend to be more emotional and volatile, be careful not to set your stops overly tight or you could be stopped out of a profitable trade prematurely. The price might retest the low (or high, as the case may be). In doing so, it could go a bit beyond the prior low or high before reversing. Many traders have a tendency to set their stop losses too narrow for gap plays. They stop out with a small loss, then miss a multiple-point move that follows. Give the stock a bit of breathing room, but if a selloff continues after a gap down, or if a run continues after a gap up, you'll want to limit losses and stop out of the trade. As previously discussed, remember that you can also limit risk by reducing your lot size. If you are frequently getting stopped out of trades prematurely, meaning you would have subsequently profited if you had not stopped out, try reducing your lot sizes so you can use wider stop-loss settings.

Know When to Hold 'Em or Fold 'Em

Equally as important as managing risk on a trade is planning how you will take profits. You've likely heard the common adages that apply to this topic: "Bulls make money; bears make money; pigs get slaughtered," and, "No one ever went broke taking profits!" If you get greedy and wait too long to take profits, you risk giving back your gains, and even worse, you risk turning a winning trade into a losing trade. Once again, this is such an important aspect of trading that in addition to discussing it here I will occasionally provide suggestions and reminders about it at other appropriate times.

As mentioned in the preceding section, taking profits is in a sense having a preplanned exit strategy for your trade. In this case, you might think of it as an exit strategy for what happens when a trade moves in your favor. I'll discuss a general approach that I frequently use for taking profits here. Chapter 10 provides other methods of planning specific entry and exit price targets that are based on technical analysis. Of course, there are many potential variations for when and how to take profits. As always, you should take the specific circumstances of a trade into consideration as well.

Many traders set hard-and-fast price targets for taking profits, and then when their price targets are hit, they close out their positions entirely. Depending on the circumstances, I may occasionally do this as well, but generally, I prefer to lock in profits a piece at a time as I achieve any significant gains. For example, suppose I buy 1,000 shares of a stock at $50 a share. If the price breaks $50.50 (the specific amount depends on the situation), I might sell half of my shares, or 500 shares in this case, and then move my stop-loss setting to break even on my remaining 500 shares, or to $50.06 in this case, allowing for commissions. This not only locks in a portion of my gains, it ensures that I can no longer lose on the trade. In other words, it ensures that a winning trade will not turn into a losing trade, which is a key rule you should strive to enforce. Ideally, you should never allow a winner to turn into a loser.

Extending the preceding example further, there are a couple of ways that I might finish out the trade, depending on how I feel about the strength of a particular trade. If I achieve additional gains but the move appears to be running out of steam, I may just take profits and close out my position entirely at that point. Alternatively, if I achieve substantial additional gains and it appears there could still be more upside movement in the play, I may once again sell half of my remaining shares and continue to trail the move with a stop-loss order, possibly tightening my stop-loss setting. At this point, I will frequently just continue trailing the move with what shares remain until the price eventually reverses and triggers my stop-loss order, thereby closing out my position. What approach works best also depends on the specifics of a given trade, the stock price, the number of shares being traded, and so on. If I have a large quantity of shares and the momentum is particularly strong in my favor, I may continue slowly taking profits off the table and stay in the trade longer. On the other hand, if there is a huge unexpected move in my favor, possibly due to breaking news or even for no apparent reason, I may just immediately take all of the gains and close out the position.

In my opinion, if a price move unexpectedly exceeds your expectations, you should take the money and run. Yes, there could be some hot news that you haven't heard about yet and you could leave money on the table, but it could just as easily go the other way and often does, so you should at least lock in a portion of your profits. After all, you are a trader. If you made money, then you did your job well, regardless of what happens after you exit the trade. And, you can always consider entering a new position later, if you subsequently discover reasons that justify doing so.

As mentioned, there are many variables to take into consideration when deciding how to take profits. The actual quantity of shares and stock prices are different for each trade. I simply used the amounts in the preceding example for illustration purposes. Obviously, if you buy a $2.00 stock rather than a $50.00 stock, you wouldn't likely wait for a 50-cent move before taking profits. Similarly, on any given trade, you might own more or less than 1,000 shares. Therefore, take the specifics of each trade into account when deciding when and how to take profits. The main points are that you must take profits when you have any significant gains, and you should never allow a winning trade to turn into a losing trade. Once you are ahead sufficiently, move your stop-loss to at least breakeven. If the price subsequently pulls back and stops you out, so be it. It's much better to stop out flat without any gain than to stop out with a loss because you didn't trail a favorable move with your stop-loss order. As you can see from reading this and the prior section about managing risk, the way you use stop-loss orders to manage risk and how you choose to take profits could determine how you exit a trade. However, you can have more specific preplanned exit strategies as well. Chapter 10 shows additional techniques you can use to plan entries, exits, and stop-loss settings for your gap trades.

Believe!

Successfully trading gaps often requires you to overcome emotions and trade contrary to what other people believe. Therefore, you should take market psychology into consideration and believe in the trend. Regardless of the initial event or news that triggers a gap, a large gap up occurs in part because people think they may miss out on a big run, so they buy impulsively. It's the reason many people will continue to buy a gap up, only to sell at a loss a short time later when, to their dismay, a snapback reversal occurs. Conversely, people panic when there is a large gap down and continue to sell rather than wait for the market to stabilize or bounce back. Trading a gap may require you to short the market when everyone else appears to be buying, or it may require you to buy long when everyone else appears to be selling. To do this, you must be able to overcome the excitement of the moment, set your emotions aside, and trust the trend.

Though a gap trend is not 100 percent (no trends are), more often than not the market will pull back when it gaps up large or will bounce when it gaps down large, even if only temporarily. Therefore, you should play the trend by shorting large gap ups, and by buying large gap downs. As previously mentioned, for modest or small gaps you should take into account all of the circumstances and use more discretion. You generally should not buy a large gap up or sell a large gap down at the open of the market. Either trade the gap trend or use the 10:00 a.m. rule as your guideline. For your convenience, here is a restatement of the 10:00 a.m. rule: If a stock gaps up, you should not buy it long unless it makes a new high after 10:00 a.m. Conversely, if a stock gaps down, you should not sell it short unless it makes a new low after 10:00 a.m.

Don't panic: You can rarely catch the exact top or bottom of a gap trade, or any trade for that matter. No one does on any kind of consistent basis. When it happens, great, but you shouldn't count on it. Therefore, you should anticipate that the trade might go against you to some degree at first. If you plan your trade using appropriate lot sizes and stop-loss cushions, you will be less likely to panic as the price fluctuates. You can relax knowing that you will stop out of the trade if it goes against you by your predefined risk limit. Additionally, with your stops in place, you will be less likely to make rash, impulsive decisions that are based on emotion rather than your original plan for the trade. As mentioned under "Managing Risk," it's best to give your stops a bit more breathing room when trading gaps because there is often some leftover buying or selling pressure initially. If necessary, you can reduce your lot size to allow for wider stop-loss settings without exceeding your maximum risk limit. When a trade does go against you and you stop out, don't beat yourself up over it! You will have both winners and losers. It was a good risk/reward play and you traded your plan. By stopping out of the trade, you preserved your capital for the next trade. As I frequently say, trading is a marathon, not a sprint. And since trading is a marathon, preserving your capital is key to succeeding over the long term.

Trading Gap Downs

As discussed earlier, a gap down occurs when a stock's price opens lower than it closed on the previous day.

The chart in Figure 8.3 of AAPL shows a gap down. Notice on the chart that AAPL gapped down by $0.84 cents, and then after a brief period of consolidation, the price of AAPL reversed direction and retraced all of the losses from the gap down, which illustrates the profit potential of fading gaps. To trade a gap down, you buy the stock long once the initial selling pressure subsides. Afterward, you should place a stop-loss order slightly beneath the low of the day, or according to your own tolerance for risk, to limit losses in the event the price continues to move lower. Chapter 10 discusses additional techniques you can consider using to time the entries and exits for your gap trades based upon charts and technical analysis.

Gap downs are powerful, high-percentage trends that provide consistent money-making opportunities. In fact, they are one of my favorite trades. During the years that I've tracked gap downs; they have been one of most consistent, profitable trends that I've used. Gap ups provide nice trading opportunities as well, but between the two, gap downs present the best opportunities. It used to be that you needed an "uptick" to short a stock, meaning the stock would have to move up for you to have the opportunity to play it short, but nowadays you can short even as a stock is falling just by placing your sale at the bid price. When playing gap downs, if you are unsure about the trade, you can wait longer for confirmation of a reversal before entering a position. And since sellers are virtually always present on gap downs, it is generally easier to enter a trade.

As before, to trade the gap down, you enter a long position once the initial selling pressure subsides, and then place a stop-loss order slightly below the low of the day, subject to your own tolerance for risk. Also notice on the chart that after the gap down reversed directions, the price continued higher and eventually surpassed the prior close. It actually moved about $2.00 from the low point of the morning. One way to take advantage of this type of move is to take profits on half of your shares once the gap fills (there is more about this in the next chapter); then you can trail any further upside movement on your remaining shares with your stop-loss order. If the upside move continues, you can continue adjusting your stop to trail it higher. If/when the price pulls back, you'll stop out of the trade with any additional gains intact.

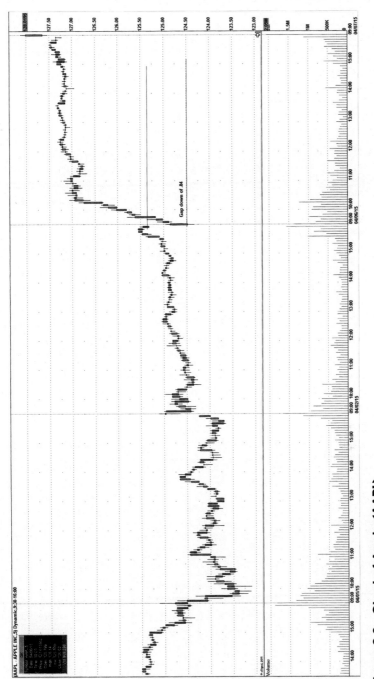

Figure 8.3 Chart of Apple (AAPL)

Trading Gap Ups

A gap up occurs when a stock's price opens higher than it closed on the previous day. The chart of Amazon (AMZN) in Figure 8.4 shows an example of a gap up. Notice that AMZN closed at $384.50 and opened the next day at $386 for a $1.50 gap up. Looking at the chart, you can see that the price reversed direction soon after AMZN opened for trading.

The price not only retraced the distance of the entire gap, it continued moving even lower. You could have faded the gap for a nice profit in a very short time frame. To trade a gap up, you sell the stock short once the initial buying pressure subsides. Afterward, you should place a stop-loss order slightly above the high of the day, or according to your own tolerance for risk, to limit losses in case the price continues to move higher. A gap reversal usually occurs within the first 30 minutes of trading. Initially, however, there may be some leftover buying interest after a gap up from people not wanting to miss out on a perceived rally. Therefore, when placing your stop-loss order, it's a good idea to leave a bit of breathing room in case the price does move slightly higher before pulling back. As mentioned earlier, due to the uptick rule you should be prepared to short into strength. You might not be able to get shares to short if you wait until the selling begins before placing an order. Although the preferred approach is to wait for signs that the buying pressure is subsiding, this is such a high-percentage trade that if the market gaps up large, with *large* being the key word, you can consider simply shorting the gap right away. If you manage risk by using a stop-loss order afterward, the potential upside reward for the trade typically outweighs the downside risk. You should use more discretion with small gaps, since price reversals are less certain. You might consider using tighter stops and reducing your lot size. When uncertain about a small or modest gap, it may be best simply to wait it out and use the 10 a.m. rule as a guideline.

The AMZN example also illustrates why it is best to give your stop losses a little breathing room, even if it means using smaller lot sizes to limit your total risk exposure. As you can see on the chart, the price initially moved higher after the gap. If you had entered the trade soon after AMZN opened for trading and your stop-loss setting

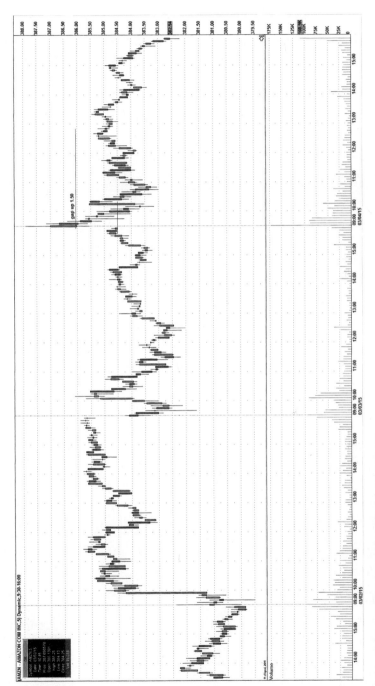

Figure 8.4 AMZN Gap Up Chart with Fade

107

was too tight, you could have potentially stopped out of the trade prematurely. If you stopped out too soon, you would have missed the price reversal and a very profitable trade. As before, to trade the gap, you would enter a short position once the buying pressure subsided. You should then place a stop-loss order slightly above the high of the day, or according to your own tolerance for risk.

CHAPTER 9

My Favorite Animal Spirits

With so many trading tools and strategies to choose among, new traders frequently ask me which I think are best. Well, I like and regularly use all of the techniques described in this book. After all, that's the reason I put them in the book. Depending on the circumstances and market conditions, each strategy has its moment in the sun, or a time when it shines bright. However, for those of you who may prefer to narrow their focus, there are a handful of techniques that have slightly edged out the others over the years to earn a spot on my list of favorites. How do they earn such an honor, you might ask? They earn it from years of consistently making my clients, and myself, the big ka-chingos!

This chapter highlights my favorite trading strategies. Although the techniques presented here are also described elsewhere in the book, I thought you might appreciate having them conveniently organized in one location for easy reference. You can look here to easily see which techniques I feel are the cream of the crop. Also, the descriptions and examples provided here differ from, or further expand upon, the corresponding material provided earlier in the book, so you might pick up a few new useful trading tidbits while reviewing them.

Although only strategies that have withstood the test of time make it onto my favorites list, I should qualify it by noting that just as the market changes over time, so may my favorite trading strategies change. If market conditions evolve such that a particular trading technique no longer works well, or it quits working for whatever reason, then I would obviously cull it from my list of favorites.

Similarly, I may discover new trends or techniques in the future that replace these but if their longevity up to this point is any indication, I suspect these strategies will continue to work their magic on my portfolio for the foreseeable future. Hopefully, they will do the same for your portfolio as well! Okay, here is the list of my favorite plays.

- Gap fades
- Earnings runs
- Earnings straddles
- FOMC fades
- 10 a.m. rule

I'll discuss each of these in greater detail and provide examples for them in the pages that follow.

Gap Fades

For good reason, gap fades are at the top of my list of favorite techniques. Fading gaps has worked consistently for me over a period of years in both bull and bear markets. I like fading both gap ups and gap downs, but between the two, fading gap downs is the winner. The further the market gaps down, the more I like the play. Since I provided a considerable amount of information earlier in the book about trading gaps, you can look there if a more detailed explanation is desired. For your convenience, I'll provide a brief review of gaps here.

A gap down occurs when the market or a stock opens lower than it closed the prior day. A gap up occurs when the market or a stock opens higher than it closed the prior day. The catalyst for gaps could be breaking news, or simply an excess of supply or demand during the trading that occurs outside of regular market hours. Since volume is low during after-hours trading, any significant buying or selling pressure can result in exaggerated price moves. Once the market opens for regular trading and volume returns to normal, these exaggerated price swings frequently correct themselves, resulting in a snapback price reversal in the direction opposite to the gap. Trading these snapback price reversals is called fading the gap. To fade a gap down, you enter a long position when the initial selling pressure subsides. To fade a gap up, you enter a short position when the initial buying pressure subsides.

Remember that there are occasions when the market gaps, then keeps on going the same direction without a snapback reversal. Therefore, to manage risk and limit potential losses, you should immediately put into place an appropriate stop-loss order after entering a gap trade. Since the market rarely opens at exactly the price that it closed the prior day, it generally gaps by some amount. On days when the gap is very small or when the market essentially opens flat, rather than fading the gap, you should hold back and wait for the market to establish a direction for the day, and as explained earlier in the book, use the 10 a.m. rule as a guideline (I'll discuss this more later in this chapter as well). You can often trade modest gaps successfully but more discretion should be used, and large gaps that are either up or down create the best trading opportunities. A chart of the Diamonds Index (DIA) in Figure 9.1 illustrates a gap down.

Looking at the chart in Figure 9.1, notice that the DIA gapped down significantly from its prior close. After the gap down, there was a brief period of consolidation where a level of support was established. To trade the gap down, you would enter a long position during the period of consolidation, or when the price breaks through the high that occurred prior to 10 a.m. Afterward, you should place a stop-loss order below the low of the day, or according to your own tolerance for risk, to limit losses in the event the market continues to move lower. If the price moves higher, you can adjust your stop-loss order accordingly and trail the upside movement, taking profits along the way as any substantial gains are achieved. At your discretion, you could take profits on all of your position, or on half of your position, then move your stop-loss to breakeven on your remaining shares. At this point, you should not lose on the trade. With profits locked in on half of your position, you can continue trailing any further upside movement on your remaining shares until you stop out of the trade.

By following this strategy with the preceding example, substantial gains were possible. As long as you didn't set your initial stop-loss setting too tight, it isn't likely you would have stopped out during the momentary pullback that took place. And if you were able to trail the move for all it was worth, you could have potentially made up to about $2-plus on the trade. Though I frequently trade individual stocks that have gapped down as well, I chose the DIA for this example. Rather than always seeking out specific stocks, I will often simply trade indexes such as the DIAs or QQQs, and so on. An advantage to using the DIA or other indexes is that unlike individual stocks,

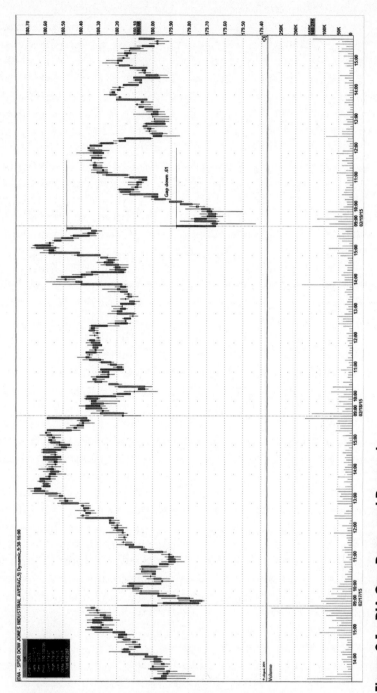

Figure 9.1 DIA Gap Down and Reversal

which don't always track the market perfectly, if the Dow bounces after a gap down, the DIA is sure to bounce as well. The DIA not only spreads risk across more than one company, it provides a true reflection of the market's price action. Conversely, with individual stocks, there are times when the market bounces and a given stock may, or may not, follow along. For example, if you buy IBM and the market bounces, IBM could bounce, remain flat, or even go down. Figure 9.2 is another example chart that shows TSLA gapping up.

To trade the gap up, you would enter a short position when the buying pressure appeared to be subsiding. Once again, you should then place a stop-loss order above the high of the day, or according to your own tolerance for risk, to limit losses in case the stock doesn't pull back as expected. As described for gap downs, you can then trail any favorable move with your stop-loss and take profits along the way at your own discretion. As you can see from the TSLA chart, gap fades provide great opportunities to trade the market on a part-time basis. So, if you can only set aside one or two hours in the mornings for trading, gap fades could provide the desired profit opportunities. I do want to make the distinction that *gap downs* are by far my favorite intraday trend—they work much better than fading gap ups in general. I often pass on gap ups unless I feel I have a very distinct advantage. I rarely pass on a gap down fade. Just sayin'!

Earnings Runs

Right next to gap *down* fades on my favorites list is earnings runs. I've charted this trend year after year, and it has been a very reliable trend, and very profitable! An earnings run trend refers to the historical tendency for the prices of popular momentum to run higher in anticipation of their earnings reports, which are commonly reported after the end of each calendar quarter. The success rate of this trend is likely over 90 percent, although that's mainly just an instinctive "gut" estimate on my part. Due to the subjective nature of such an effort, and the fact that the best stocks to play changes on a quarterly basis, I haven't tried to precisely calculate the percentage. However, I've tracked this trend for years and I can attest that it virtually always works at some level.

As always, you should take into account overall market conditions, and any sector- or stock-specific circumstances when evaluating

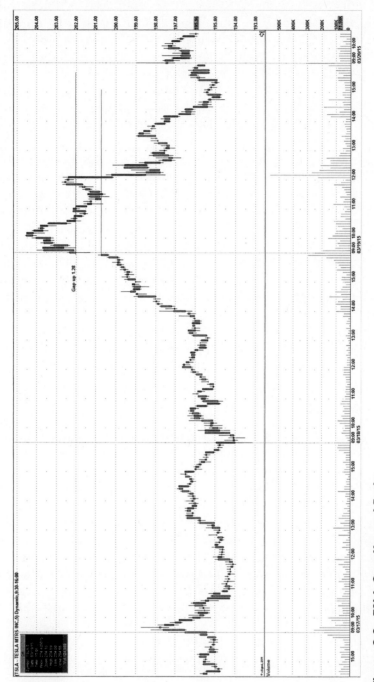

Figure 9.2 TSLA Gap Up and Fade

the potential for earnings to run at the end of any given quarter. Depending on overall market sentiment, the strength and timing of an earnings run can vary. If the market at large is weak going into earnings season, an earrings run may occur a week or so later than usual. If the market has already run up substantially and is in an over-bought condition going into earnings, the earnings trend could be somewhat weaker as a result. In some instances, the market overall might be moving sideways or appear to be weak on the surface while individual momentum stocks are still running up ahead of their earnings reports. Other earnings run variations are possible as well.

A potentially good setup for an earnings run occurs when the market pulls back, creating a slightly oversold condition, just ahead of earnings season. Under ideal conditions, the upside potential for an earnings run can be explosive. The main point is that the precise timing and strength of earnings runs can vary, but there is generally at least some subset of individual momentum companies that run up ahead of their earnings. In general, individual momentum stocks tend to start running up about two weeks ahead of their scheduled earnings report. Of course, as I discussed earlier, this is based on the overall historical patterns of various stocks and sectors. On any given quarter, you need to consider overall market conditions and the historical patterns for the specific stocks you are trading, and make any appropriate adjustments.

To find potential trading candidates, you can review online earnings calendars for companies that are scheduled to report earnings in the coming weeks. Various online news and stock market oriented services provide earnings calendars. A word of caution about earnings calendars, however: Use discretion because not all are created with the same due diligence, and some may contain inaccurate information. Additionally, companies sometimes change the date of their earnings reports, and services that do not regularly confirm the earnings dates may not reflect these last-minute changes. This is important because a key rule to trading the earnings trend is that you exit your position ahead of the actual earnings report, and if you are basing the timing of your exit on inaccurate information, it could be a very costly mistake.

Once you find some potential stocks to trade, you can pull up charts and research them to determine how they behaved ahead of their earnings reports in the past. I typically go back a couple of years to confirm the trend. If a stock has only run up once or twice in a row, though it may be of interest, I don't consider it a solid trend. Three times could potentially establish an early trend, and I'd consider more than that to be indicative of a trend. Basically, the more times the trend repeats itself, the better. And though an occasional miss doesn't necessarily break the trend, you should use reasonable discretion and watch it more closely. Since news rules, before entering a trade you should also check the latest news for each individual stock and their sectors to be certain nothing is going on that could adversely impact an earnings run. Figure 9.3 is a chart of AAPL that shows how it traded leading into an earnings report. We actually traded this stock for an earnings run.

Looking at the chart 9.3, notice the sideways consolidation action that occurred during the weeks that preceded the earnings season. Basing action such as this often provides a great setup for an earnings play entry. You can enter a position when you see an upside break of the range, or if you feel the trend for a given stock is particularly strong and can tolerate slightly more risk, you could even enter the trade during the basing period and place a stop-loss order just under the support level of the range.

Another reason I like this trade is because it was lagging other similar stocks that were already running up ahead of their earnings. We entered the trade as buying interest in the stock picked up. We sold AAPL on the day of its earnings report, which is a key rule for playing an earnings trend. I don't recommend holding a stock into its actual earnings report, even when you expect a positive earnings report. In my opinion, that is gambling, since there is no way to be certain in advance what will come out in the earnings report. If earnings are bad, or a company warns or lowers estimates for future earnings, you might not only give back any gains you've achieved, but you could incur substantial losses. In this case AAPL moved much higher post-earnings, but trust me, you don't want to be on the wrong end of a bad earnings report!

Additionally, stocks that have had a large upside move ahead of earnings will frequently sell off after their earnings report, even when the report is positive. It's often a case of buy the rumor and sell the news. Although there are times when a company will blow out earnings and run higher, to me the upside potential isn't worth the risk. To play an earnings run trend, you should enter a position as

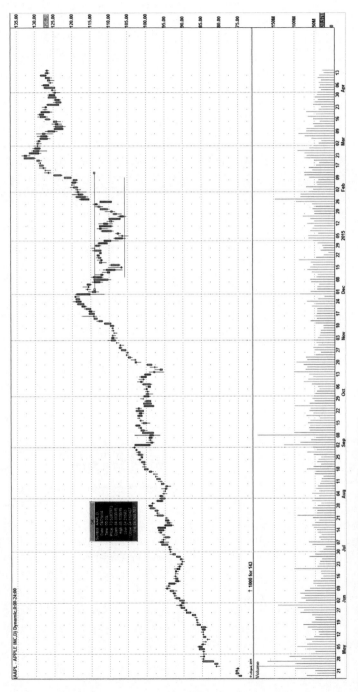

Figure 9.3　Chart of AAPL into Earnings 2015

appropriate ahead of a company's earnings report and exit the position on the day of the report before the market closes, or at your own discretion, even sooner. Meaning, whenever substantial gains are achieved, you can take some or all of your profits sooner. Similarly, if the risk/reward for a trade changes and is no longer favorable, possibly due to breaking news or for whatever reason, you may want to exit a position early to limit losses.

As I've mentioned, my preference is to take profits along the way as I achieve any substantial gains, and that applies to earnings runs as well. What I will often do is sell half of my position, and then move my stop-loss to break even on my remaining shares. This locks in profits and ensures that I can't lose on the trade. Then, I will trail any further upside movement with my stop-loss order and take profits at my own discretion, or I'll simply continue trailing the move until I stop out of the trade. Figure 9.4 is another earnings run example that shows the price action for GOOG ahead of an earnings report. In this case, we used options to play the earnings run as well because the stock is obviously very high priced and the only way I will typically play a stock over $100 (or even $50 often) is using options; it limits my risk and I can still max out my upside percentage-wise.

As you can see on Figure 9.4, GOOG had a nice run during the two weeks that preceded its earnings report. Earnings were on January 29, so you can see it went literally $30+! That's a pretty freakin' nice trade, eh? Once again, notice the basing action that preceded the run. At this point, I was watching the stock closely as a potential earnings run candidate. As I noticed, activity picking up near the end of the basing period, I took advantage of a brief pullback to enter a position about 10 days out from earnings. I not only played the stock for the earnings run, I decided to use options for the play as well. Not only did options let me clearly predefine my risk, the premiums were sufficiently attractive that I saw the potential for huge gains if the stock ran into earnings. As always, risk versus reward should play a big part in any trade equation.

If you can find a small cap, as shown in Figure 9.5, you can make a small killing when you're right. We played Plug Power (PLUG) for earnings and the beast went medieval on the market. In the next chapter, I'll go over *breakouts* and *breakdowns* and show you why I consider these trading strategies golden geese.

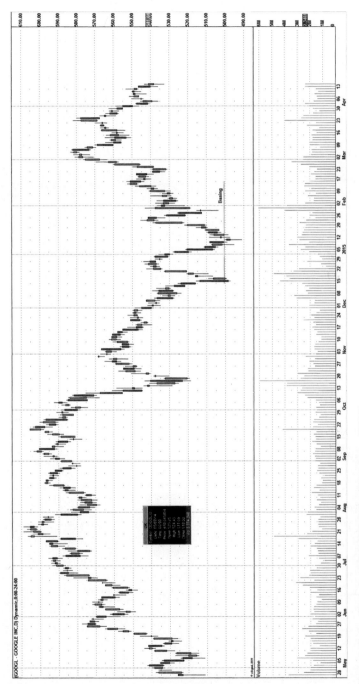

Figure 9.4 Chart of GOOG into Earnings 2015

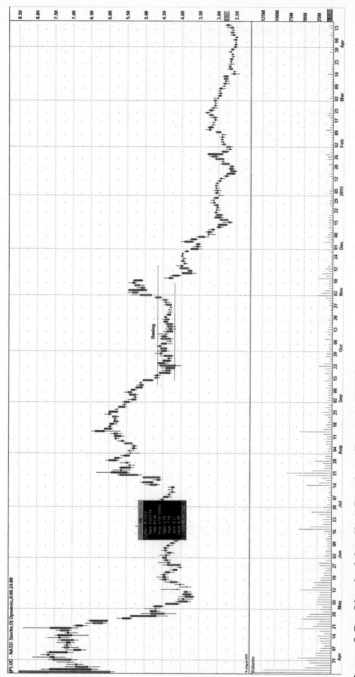

Figure 9.5 Chart of Another Earnings Runner (PLUG)

Earnings Straddles

Another consistently profitable, and therefore favorite, technique I like to use to play earnings runs is option straddles. Though this is based on the same earnings run trend that I just discussed, it employs a different strategy that uses options to play the trend. To clarify—a straddle is a technique you can use to potentially profit from a large move in a stock's price, regardless of whether the move is up or down. To put on a straddle, you buy both *call* and *put* options at the same strike price for the same expiration month.

When playing an earnings straddle, rather than always selling prior to an earnings report, which I will still do if I achieve the desired gains, I may hold the trade or a portion of it over the earnings report. In this case, since your risk is already predefined and limited, if you don't yet have sufficient gains to profit on the trade, you can hold it over the earnings report and potentially profit from large earnings-related price moves. In fact, if the option premiums are particularly low, I will sometimes speculate on the actual earnings report using options by putting on a straddle the day a company is scheduled to report earnings.

An earnings option straddle has been a high percentage play for me over the years. In other words, the risk/reward for the play has been great! A key element of the trade is getting into the straddle at a favorable total premium. With that in mind, I usually play earnings option straddles for companies that are reporting earnings during the last week of options expirations. Since the time-based component of option premiums is lowest at this time, and the spreads between the two option positions are tighter, it's more likely that I can put on a straddle at a favorable total cost. To profit on a straddle, you need the underlying stock's price to move a sufficiently large amount in a short period of time. Earnings runs and earnings reports generate the desired volatility for such potentially sharp price swings. In an ideal situation, you might even get the opportunity to roll out of both sides of the trade with a profit. Figure 9.6 is a chart of Netflix (NFLX) the day of earnings, and the day after.

Generally when you play a straddle, you try to set up the position without a bias in either direction. Meaning, both sides of the trade are roughly the same value, and the strike price is roughly the same as the underlying stock's price. When this isn't the case, there is a built-in bullish or bearish bias to some degree, where you either make

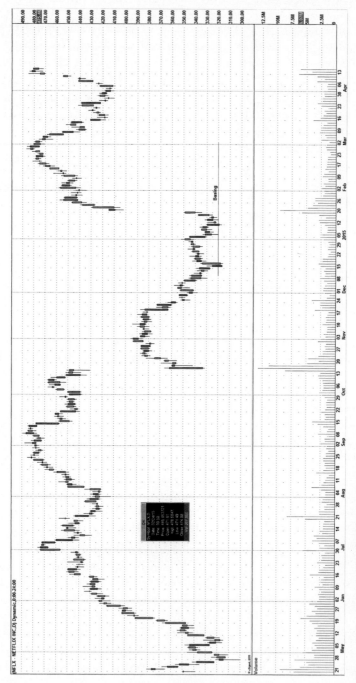

Figure 9.6 Chart of NFLX 2015 Earnings

or lose more when the price moves in one direction or the other. In some instances, this can work to your advantage if you actually desire a bias going into the trade. In the case of the NFLX, clearly if you had a positive bias, you'd have made *big* ka-chingos! Now with NFLX, the cost of the straddle was *huge*; you would have had to pay about a $25 premium. The risk is that NFLX doesn't move more than $25 in either direction, in which case you could conceivably lose your entire play. However, after a positive earnings report, the stock moved *very* dramatically. No strategy works all the time, but if you use proper money management, you don't need them to work all the time, not even close! In fact, a good trader can hit on 40 percent and make money in my experience. Hey, even a monkey throwing darts will hit 50 percent!

FOMC Fades

Another technique that I like is fading FOMC (Federal Open Market Committee) announcements. As explain in Chapter 13, the FOMC is a 12-member committee that is responsible for setting interest rate and credit policies. When the FOMC meets the market often becomes uncertain and anxious about the outcome of the meeting. Will interest rates go up, go down, or remain the same? Will the Fed change its future interest rate bias, loosen or tighten their monetary policy, or make other comments about the state of the economy that could impact the market?

Whether it's justified or not, the market tends to react dramatically to the FOMC news releases. Depending on the announcement, sometimes the reactions are only momentary, sometimes they last the rest of day, and sometimes they carry over into subsequent days or weeks. Regardless of the overall duration of the impact on the market, immediately after the FOMC announcement the market is typically very volatile and behaves erratically for a period of time as traders digest the news (I'll provide a chart illustration of this a bit later). On some occasions, the Dow moves by 100 points or more in one direction, and then abruptly swings back in the other direction by the same amount. In extreme instances, all of this can take place in a matter of minutes—particularly in cases where there is confusion initially about the significance or meaning of an FOMC announcement. Eventually the market digests the news and begins to settle down or establish a clearer directional trend. Although the price action can be fast paced and may require some agility, the initial volatility that follows an FOMC meeting announcement presents a great trading opportunity for traders that anticipate it. Though not always, more often than not the first impulsive move that follows the FOMC announcement is exaggerated, and perhaps more importantly, it's often based on irrational, emotional trading.

As I related earlier, the fade is a very strong trend, but it's the third move, which these days is usually in the original move's direction, and is the one that can be the strongest. Therefore, similar to playing gap reversals, I generally fade the first impulsive move that occurs after an FOMC announcement, then fade that move into the close. Actually, the move is frequently so impulsive that it typically results in a sharp spike on a chart. The larger the first spike is, the better. Even in cases where the direction of the first impulse doesn't turn out to be incorrect, by fading the move I'm betting that it will at least be exaggerated initially and will snap back in the other direction as a result, or that it will simply fade the other way to some degree due to the initial confusion caused by the announcement. Either way, you can potentially profit from the trade even if a corrective snap-back reversal is only temporary. To fade an FOMC announcement, I like to use volatile momentum stocks that are in volatile sectors. As an example, the chart in Figure 9.7 shows how AAPL reacted to an FOMC announcement.

The outcome of an FOMC meeting is usually announced about 2:00 p.m. EST. It's a good idea to watch a business news channel such as CNBC for the announcement, in addition to keeping an eye on your online news service. Looking at the chart, notice the price moved lower in anticipation of the announcement. After the announcement, there was a sharp upward price spike, which was immediately followed by a snapback price reversal. The open/white candlestick bar on the chart indicates the *upside* spike, and the very next light bar indicates the reversal, and then the next green bar indicates the fade of that move. The whole process was over in a matter of a few minutes. Also note the overall amount of volatility surrounding the FOMC announcement.

To fade the reversal, you would enter a short position on the first upside spike and exit the position upon achieving gains from the reversal. Then you could, as we did, enter a fade of that fade and ride it to the close. As you can see on the chart, the price action can be quite rapid so you need to be prepared to act quickly. Additionally, you

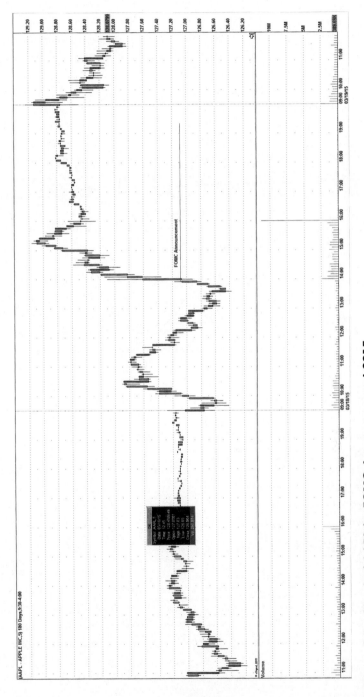

Figure 9.7 Chart of AAPL for FOMC Announcement 2015

really need a direct-access brokerage account to reliably trade this trend. Web-based platforms generally don't have sufficient execution speeds to ensure you can get in and out of the trade quickly enough, and reliably. In fact, the price action for this play is sometimes so fast that it is one of the rare situations where I have occasionally used a market order during the first spike to help ensure that I don't miss the reversal. Since I want to catch the bottom of the move for a reversal, anyway, a market order will generally fill somewhere near that point. However, I must stress that you should only use a market order if you have a fast direct-access trading platform and understand what you are doing.

Using the preceding example, if your trading platform is too slow or your timing isn't correct, a market order could fill after the reversal near the price top or bottom, rather than at a favorable price prior to the reversal. Referring to the chart once again, you can see that in this case the price action settled down a short time later, then resumed its prior trend for the duration of the day, which was essentially a nice *big* upside move. The prior trend doesn't always resume, as in this case. Depending on the FOMC news, a rally or selloff could endure after the initial reaction. If the initial spike after an FOMC announcement was to the downside rather than the upside, you would simply reverse the process previously described and enter a long position rather than a short position. In addition to using stocks for the FOMC fade, I'll frequently buy Diamond (DIA) options, or options on another index such as the XLF or BHP, or USO, but you tend to get a cleaner move with the market. (I discussed using index options in more detail under the "Gap Fades.") However, you should only use limit orders when fading an FOMC move with options. You could easily get filled at a very unfavorable price attempting to use market orders with fast-moving index options.

10:00 a.m. Rule Plays

I'm including the 10:00 a.m. rule in my list of favorites because it has proven to be a reliable indicator as to the near-term direction of the market, or individual stocks. Following the 10:00 a.m. rule has not only proven to be a consistently profitable strategy, it has also helped many traders avoid losses from entering trades prematurely. Though I covered the 10:00 a.m. rule earlier in the book, for your convenience, here it is again.

If a stock gaps up, you should not buy it long unless it makes a new high after 10:00 a.m. Conversely, if a stock gaps down, you should not sell it short unless it makes a new low after 10:00 a.m. The 10:00 a.m. rule concept is actually very straightforward. Using the 10:00 a.m. rule, if a stock you are watching for a trade setup makes a new high after 10:00 a.m., you could buy it for a long trade. Conversely, if a stock makes a new low after 10:00 a.m., you could sell it short for a trade. For example, suppose MSFT opened for trading at $42.00, and then between 9:30 a.m. and 10:00 a.m., it made a high of $42.35. If at any time after 10:00 a.m. the price hits $42.36, you could conceivably buy it long for a trade. As always is the case, you still need to consider overall market conditions and other circumstances applicable to a given stock, but as long as these are conducive for the trade, you could potentially profit by entering a long position since a new high after 10:00 a.m. is a bullish indicator. Alternatively, using the preceding example, suppose MSFT opened at $42.00 then made a low of $41.70 between 9:30 a.m. and 10:00 a.m. If it subsequently hit $41.69 after 10:00 a.m., you could conceivably short it for a trade since a new low after 10:00 a.m. is a bearish indicator. Once again, this assumes that any other applicable factors are conducive for the trade.

How or Why Does the 10:00 a.m. Rule Work?

Well, when the market first opens for the day there tends to be more emotional trading and uncertainty. The market hasn't yet found its footing or established any type of directional bias, and worse, it could send false signals as to its true direction. Plus, there is frequently pent-up demand on either the buy side or the sell side initially due to leftover imbalances from post- and pre-market trading. All of these issues are usually resolved by 10:00 a.m., so the price action that occurs after 10:00 a.m. is generally a more reliable indicator of the true directional bias of the market. Hence, the 10:00 a.m. rule was created. It provides guidelines not only to help avoid the early morning pitfalls but also to potentially achieve greater profits, especially on directional trending days.

Figure 9.8 is a chart of Alibaba (BABA) that illustrates the 10:00 a.m. rule. Notice that the market initially began the day where it left off the prior day, essentially opening flat. Shortly after 10:00 a.m., BABA broke through its pre–10:00 a.m. high. At this point, you could enter a long position. You should then place a

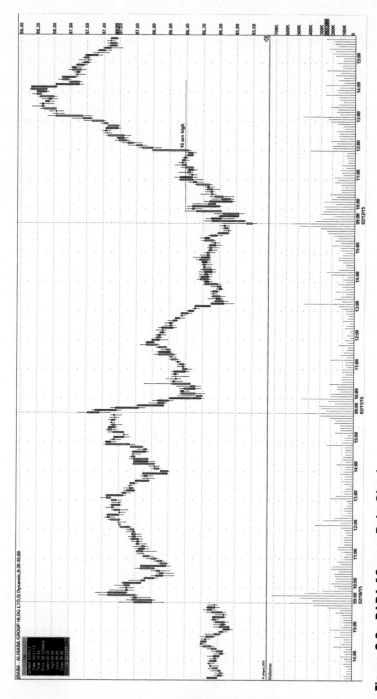

Figure 9.8   BABA 10 a.m. Rule Chart

stop-loss order slightly beneath the low that occurred prior to 10:00 a.m. If the market subsequently reverses directions, you should limit your losses by stopping out of the trade. In the preceding example, you could have profited nicely on the trade by following the 10 a.m. rule. As the price moves higher, you should continue to trail the move with your stop-loss order. And as I've discussed before, my preference is to take profits along the way as any substantial gains are achieved. Once sufficient gains are achieved, I'll frequently take profits on half of my position and then move my stop-loss to breakeven on my remaining shares. At this point, I can no longer lose on the trade. Next, I typically trail any additional gains on my remaining shares, either until I stop out of the trade, or until I decide to take any additional profits and exit the position.

Figure 9.9 shows another example of the 10:00 a.m. rule that illustrates a move to the downside using Bank of America (BAC). Note that BAC gapped up initially. As you can see, anyone who got caught up in the initial buying frenzy and went long paid the price a short time later. This serves as an example of how the 10:00 a.m. rule can help prevent premature trade entries, which is great when they would have been on the wrong side of the trade. By following the 10:00 a.m. rule, either you would fade the gap up or you would sell short once the stock made a new low after 10:00 a.m. Upon entering a position, you should then place a stop-loss order slightly above the high that occurred prior to 10:00 a.m., which in this case would be about $16.60. Afterward, you would continue to trail any substantial gains and take profits along the way, as described for the previous example. Once again, you could have achieved nice gains by using the 10:00 a.m. rule as a guideline for timing a short entry. Of course, these examples are only for illustration purposes. There are days when the market briefly makes a new high or low after 10:00 a.m. and subsequently moves sideways or reverses direction. In the case of reversals, your stop-loss orders will trigger and limit potential losses, which is why it is important to use stop-losses. On range-bound days, whether you profit on the trade and by how much would obviously depend on the specifics of the trade and the size of the trading range. Generally, the best gains are achieved when the market establishes a directional trend that lasts for the entire day. That's when you can make the really big ka-chingos!

Figure 9.10 is a *gap and go* for Facebook (FB) where you can see the stock gapped up and kept making highs throughout the day.

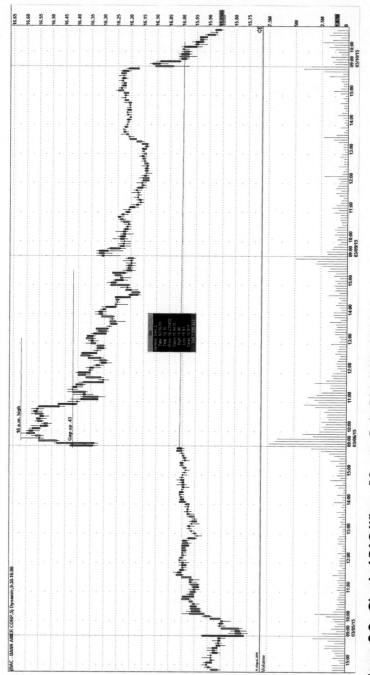

Figure 9.9   Chart of BAC Where 10 a.m. Rule Didn't Work! 2015

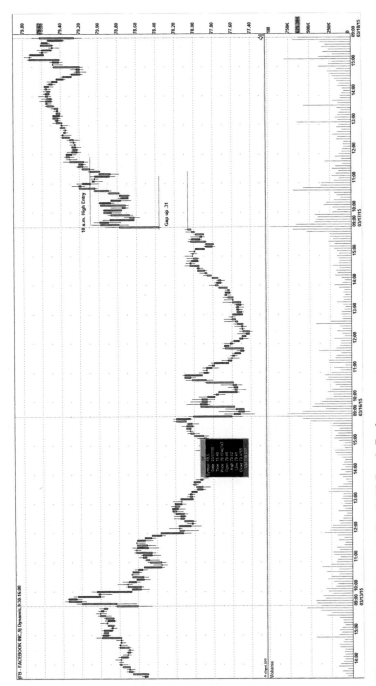

Figure 9.10 FB Gap and Go Until Day's End

If you bought on the 10:00 a.m. rule breakout, you did A-OK! And, let's say you actually faded it short at the open on the *gap up*. So you stop out at 10 a.m. highs and then reenter *long* on same break, if you like. Yeah, you'd have lost a little on the fade, but you'd have more than made up for it on the breakout long. Again, keep in mind that these ideas don't always work, but by planning your trade and trading your plan, you give yourself a potentially huge advantage and edge—and baby, that's all we can really ask for!

CHAPTER 10

Trading Gaps Using Technical Analysis

In addition to the approaches described in Chapter 8, you can use charts and technical analysis to help determine entry and exit price targets for your gap trades. This chapter describes many of these techniques, but before continuing, I would like to point out that I often don't use technical analysis to trade gaps. Although I do occasionally use charts for additional confirmation of a gap trade, in cases where there is a large gap down and I'm confident about the trade, I will frequently just buy the gap right at the open as described in Chapter 8 rather than wait for confirmation using technical analysis. Conversely, if I'm shorting a large gap up, I might even short a stock during premarket trading. Large gaps are such powerful, high-percentage trends that I generally don't feel the need to wait for technical confirmation. However, many traders prefer to use technical analysis to help pick their entry and exit points, so for those of you who might have such an interest I'm including a variety of charting techniques that are useful for trading gaps. The following strategies help you pick exact entry and exit points for your trades, but which techniques to use is really a matter of personal preference and what works best for you. You'll likely find that as you gain more experience and develop your own intuition about trading gaps, you'll discover other shortcuts and tricks to use in addition to these.

Reversal Bars

Reversal bars, or candles, are just a few among many well-known candlestick chart formations that are used when performing technical analysis. They frequently signal a change of trend is on the way. Since some of the sections that follow employ the use of reversal bars to set entry and exit price targets for gap trades, for your convenience, a brief introduction to reversal bars is provided here. Just keep in mind that technical analysis and candlestick charting involves much more than is practical to include here for gap trading purposes. Also keep in mind, I'm not an expert chartist. I don't use them that often, and when I do I usually ask my partner, Mike Di Gioia, or someone else who is an expert what they think. If you would like to explore technical analysis and/or candlestick charting further, there are many good books devoted entirely to these topics.

Doji

The appearance of a doji candle (see Figure 10.1) indicates the price opened and closed within a tight range for the candle's time period (I generally use 5 minutes when trading gaps). It means the bulls and bears were in a tug of war. If a stock has been in a directional trend, either up or down, a doji could signal a potential change of direction is on the way. Dojis are very powerful indicators. When you see one, you should at least consider it a red flag. Some traders will even enter a trade or tighten stops, based solely on seeing a doji, particularly when a stock has been in a strong directional trend up to that point.

(Arm and) Hammer

A hammer has a very small stub as the upper shadow (the thin line above and below the rectangular body of the candle), and a long

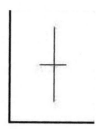

Figure 10.1   Chart Showing Doji

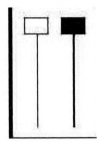

Figure 10.2   Chart Showing Hammer

lower shadow as shown in Figure 10.2. It has a short real body that is positioned at the top of the candle. A hammer is another powerful indicator of strong support, and often indicates the end of a significant downtrend. Confirmation occurs when the price breaks above the top of the hammer. While you don't necessarily want to jump in and trade a hammer when in a sideways range, in a downtrend it is a great low-risk, high-percentage trade, especially when it occurs at a support level. You can enter a long position with defined risk by buying a break of the high of the hammer and putting a stop-loss order just below the bottom of the hammer.

Shooting Star

A shooting star looks like an upside-down hammer, or inverted hammer (see Figure 10.3). It has a long upper shadow with a short, stubby shadow underneath. A shooting star is a powerful bearish indicator, and a very reliable indicator of an uptrend reversal.

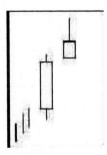

Figure 10.3   Chart Showing Shooting Star

When to Enter

Following are a variety of technical analysis strategies that you may find useful for timing the entries to gap trades. After the entry strategies are explained, exit strategies are also discussed.

First Bar High/Low Entry

One entry technique for trading gaps is to use the high and low of the first bar of an intraday chart. The high is used to set an entry for gap downs, and the low is used for gap ups. Though some traders use 1-minute or 3-minute charts, I've achieved better results trading gaps with 5-minute charts. Therefore, I generally use 5-minute charts. Figure 10.4 is a 5-minute intraday candlestick chart of ARMH that shows a gap down. Notice on the chart that the high price of the first bar after the gap down is $48.80 (see Figure 10.5 for a closeup view of the bars). If the stock's price breaks the high of the first bar, or moves higher than 48.80 in this case, it's a sign of buying interest, which indicates the gap down could be reversing. Therefore, you could use $49.40 as an entry price target for the trade, as that's where it fills the gap. Here is a closeup view of the first two candlestick bars that followed the gap down on the preceding chart. You would buy the stock long when the price reaches $48.80 and then place a stop-loss order slightly beneath the low of the first bar, which is generally the low of the day as well. The chart in Figure 10.5 shows another first bar entry based on a gap down of MSFT.

Since the high of the first bar after the gap down on the preceding MSFT chart is $40.82, you could enter the trade long once the price hits $40.83, and then place a stop-loss order slightly beneath the low of the first bar. You can also use the first bar to determine entry targets for gap ups. In the case of gap ups, you simply reverse the process and sell short when the price breaks through the low of the first bar. You would then place your stop-loss order slightly above the high of the first bar.

Inside Bar Entry

Another way you can set an entry price target for a gap trade is by using an inside bar, shown in Figure 10.6. An inside bar occurs when a bar's high price is lower than the previous bar's high, and its low is higher than the previous bar's low. The price range of an inside bar is "inside" the range of the prior bar, as shown in Figure 10.7.

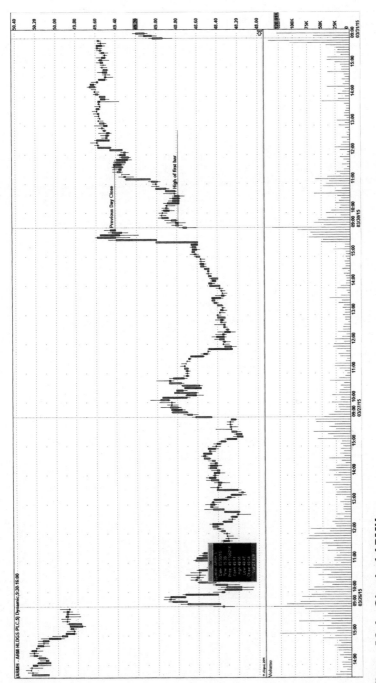

Figure 10.4 Chart of ARMH

137

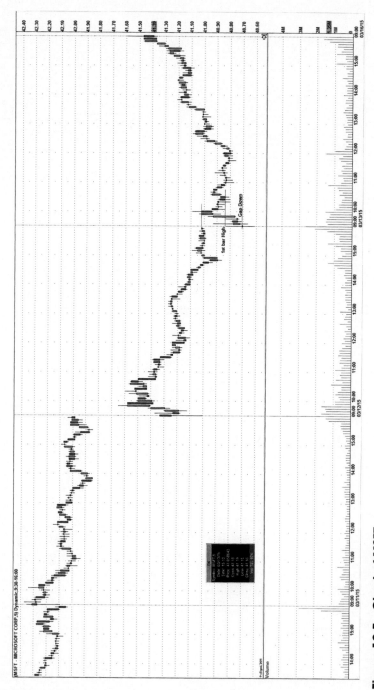

Figure 10.5 Chart of MSFT

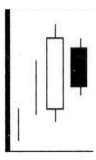

Figure 10.6   Chart of Inside Bar

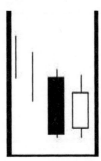

Figure 10.7   Chart Inside Bar—Price Range "Inside"

Inside bars indicate contracting range and volatility, which also indicates the selling pressure is subsiding. And as mentioned earlier, since emotions also play a role in causing stocks to gap, inside bars can indicate that the emotional selling may be coming to an end. The chart of OIH in Figure 10.8 shows how an inside bar can be used to set an entry price target for a gap down trade.

Inside bars are my favorite indicators for determining entry targets when I'm using technical analysis confirmation of gaps. I particularly like inside bars when the bars that precede the inside bar are trending in the direction of the gap, as in the preceding example. Meaning, the gap is to the downside and the bars preceding the inside bar are trending downward as well. Inside bars are such powerful indicators that I generally don't wait for any additional technical confirmation after seeing one (e.g., like a break of the first bar's high). You can set your entry price target slightly above the high of the inside bar. In the prior example, the inside bar price range is from $33.53 to $33.63 so you could enter the trade long when the price hits $33.64. Upon entering the trade, place a stop-loss order

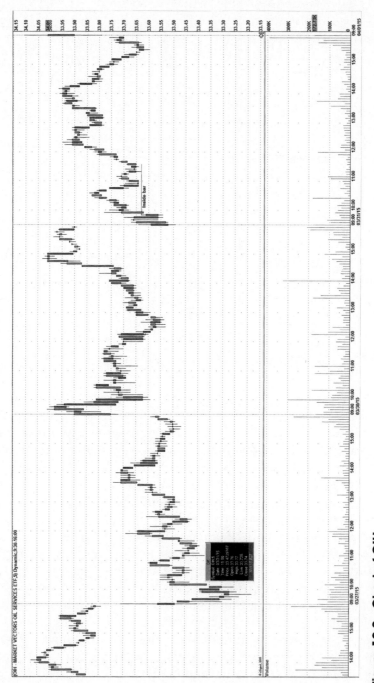

Figure 10.8 Chart of OIH

slightly beneath the low of the inside bar to limit your risk should the trade go against you. Should the inside bar's low be too close (and unreasonably narrow) for a stop-loss order, you can consider using the lowest low of the bars that preceded the inside bar, or the low of the day. See the "Using Stops" section later in this chapter for additional stop-loss guidelines and suggestions. Inside bars can also be used to trade gap ups. Figure 10.9 shows a gap up of FCAU.

Notice on the chart in Figure 10.9 that the first bar's price ranges from $X to $Y. The next bar is an inside bar, because its range of $X to $Y is inside the range of the first bar. Since this is a gap up, the price target is just under the low of the inside bar, or $X, which in this case just happens to be the low of the first bar as well. If the price hits $Y, you could sell the stock short and then place a stop-loss order slightly above the bar's high, or once again, you can consider using another nearby level of resistance in situations where you might need to widen your stop slightly.

Reversal Bars

You can also use reversal bar formations to set entry price targets for gap trades, although this strategy does tend to be a bit more aggressive. Figure 10.10 is a chart of Netflix (NFLX) that shows a shooting star reversal bar, which appeared soon after the stock gapped up.

As mentioned earlier, a shooting star often signals the end of an uptrend, or a gap up, in this case. Looking at Figure 10.10, notice that the price fell a short time after the appearance of the shooting star. Upon seeing a shooting star after a gap up, you could sell the stock short when the price breaks through the low of the shooting star. After entering a position, place your stop-loss order just above the high of the shooting star. When using reversal bars, your stop-losses should generally be fairly tight. If the indicator fails, which is the case if the price subsequently breaks the high of the preceding shooting star, you should stop out of the trade. A related tidbit that you can keep in mind is that another potential trading opportunity occurs when a pattern formation fails. You can frequently enter a profitable trade in the opposite direction based on the failure of a pattern setup. Stocks in similar businesses or sectors will often move in sympathy with one another. Bad news came out about Priceline (PCLN), which is in a similar business as Expedia (EXPE), so EXPE also gapped down on the bad news.

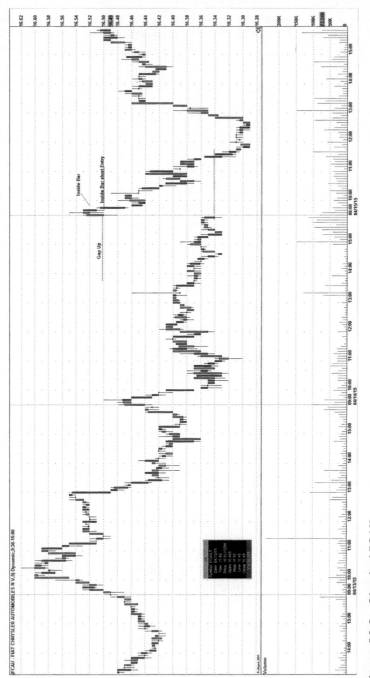

Figure 10.9 Chart of FCAU

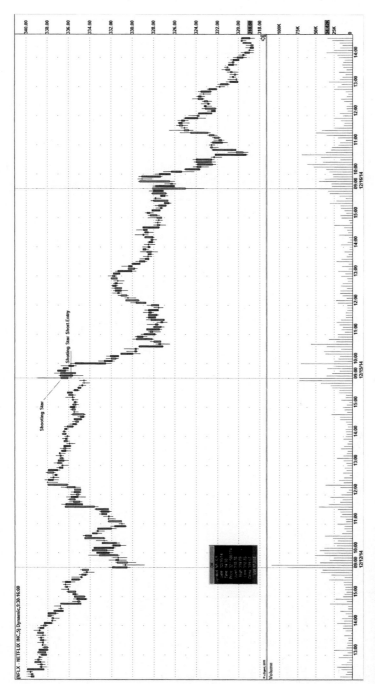

Figure 10.10　NFLX Chart

Figure 10.11 illustrates a trade entry that is based on a hammer reversal bar. Here is a closeup view of the hammer reversal bar. As discussed earlier, a hammer frequently signals the end of a downtrend. Notice EXPE was initially trending lower after the gap down. Shortly after the hammer appeared, the stock reversed direction and moved higher. You could set a potential entry price target just above the high of the hammer reversal bar. If the price breaks through the high of the hammer, then there is a good chance the downtrend may be reversing. After entering a position, you would

Figure 10.11   Closeup on Hammer Reversal

place a stop-loss order slightly beneath the low of the reversal bar. As before, if the reversal bar fails, you should limit losses and exit the trade.

The OOPS Entry

Larry Williams, a systems/commodity trader, coined the term "OOPS" and invented the OOPS setup in the 1970s, though his usage of the setup includes more variations than presented here for our purposes. He noticed when the market gaps up, people tend to get caught up in the buying frenzy and continue to buy the gap up; then when the selling begins, they realize the mistake with an "OOPS," so he called the setup "OOPS"! An OOPS setup occurs when a gap up opens higher than the previous day's high price, rather than simply opening higher than the previous day's closing price, or, conversely, in the case of a gap down, when the price opens lower than the previous day's low price, rather than its closing price. Actually, if a gap is strictly defined from a technical point of view, true gaps are very straight forward. That is, a gap up is when the price opens higher than the previous day's high, and a gap down is when the price opens lower than the previous day's low. When a gap is based on the closing price only, and doesn't exceed the prior high or low, as the case may be, it is technically referred to as a *lap*. Still, most people refer to either as a gap, and I generally do as well. However, for the purpose of discussing an OOPS entry, it seemed appropriate to make the distinction. In the case of a gap up, an OOPS entry price target is the breach of the prior day's high. And for a gap down, it is a breach of the prior day's low. The YHOO chart in Figure 10.12 shows an OOPS gap up that provides two potential entry targets, an inside bar entry and an OOPS entry.

Referring to the chart 10.12, notice that the following day, GOOGLE opened higher than the prior high. Therefore, it is a potential OOPS trading opportunity. The OOPS entry target is just below the prior day's high. Also, though, the second bar that appears is an inside bar. While you could wait for an OOPS entry, my preference in this case would be to take the inside bar entry. As explained earlier, for an inside bar the entry for a gap up is just below the inside bar's low. Therefore, to trade off of the inside bar target, you would sell the stock short when the price hits breaks below the lows. Then, place a stop-loss order above the inside bar's high, or above another

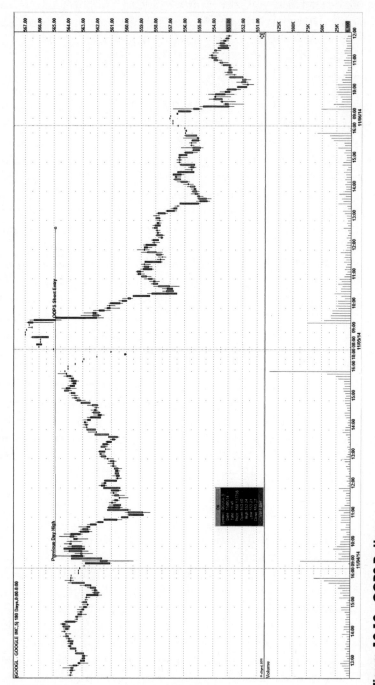

Figure 10.12 OOPS Pattern

nearby area of resistance if the stop seems unreasonably narrow. In such cases, it's likely the stop would be just above the highest high of one of the bars immediately preceding the inside bar. If you miss the inside bar entry, or prefer to wait for the OOPS entry, you would sell the stock short when the price hits the OOPS entry price target, using the preceding example.

The official point to set a stop-loss order for an OOPS trade is the high of the day. However, the high of the day can sometimes be a fairly wide stop, which is one reason I'm not a big fan of the official OOPS trade. In my opinion, you should take into account your tolerance for risk, the circumstances of the gap, and the price action ahead of the trade to determine the best setting for your stop-loss order. If the range is not too wide, you could use the official recommendation and set a stop slightly above the high of the day. Otherwise, I would look for a closer area of resistance, or once I had gains, I would take profits prior to a price pullback. Another risk management alternative is to reduce your lot size so that a wider stop remains within range of your maximum risk limit. Regardless of the approach, I think it's important to predetermine the amount of risk you are willing to accept on any trade, and then adjust the parameters of a trade to stay within that limit. Capital preservation is key to succeeding long term as a trader. A gap down OOPS trade works exactly the same as for a gap up, except in reverse. The OOPS entry target is a breach to the upside of the prior day's low, in which case, you would buy the stock long and use the current day's low for the official stop-loss placement. Once again, I recommend an approach that narrows the stop-loss setting when the daily low falls outside of your maximum risk tolerance for a trade.

Gap and Goooooooooo!!!

Though in most cases if the market gaps large, there is a snapback price reversal, there are also days when the market gaps and just keeps on going in the same direction. I call this gap and go. How do you trade gap-and-go days? These are the days that you use the 10:00 a.m. rule. For your convenience, here is a brief restatement of the 10:00 a.m. rule. If a stock gaps up, you should not buy it long unless it makes a new high after 10:00 a.m. Conversely, if a stock gaps down, you should not sell it short unless it makes a new low after

10:00 a.m. Following the 10:00 a.m. rule, if a stock gaps up and then makes a new high after 10:00 a.m., you would buy the stock long.

The Alkermes (ALKS) chart in Figure 10.13 shows an example of this type of entry. Notice that after ALKS gapped up, rather than reversing, the price continued to move higher. This is an indication that buying pressure is increasing, and/or selling pressure is subsiding. The high prior to 10:00 a.m. is what we use to set the range's high value. When those highs are breached you could enter a long position. Afterward, you should place a stop-loss order slightly beneath the low that occurred prior to 10:00 a.m. If this would result in a stop-loss that is too wide and outside of your maximum risk limit, adjust your stop or lot size such that your maximum risk isn't exceeded (possibly to another nearby support level). Later in this chapter, the "Using Stops" section provides additional stop-loss guidelines and suggestions. In the preceding example, you can see that an entry based on a breach of the high that occurred prior to 10:00 a.m. resulted in a nice short-term trade. Another gap-up-and-go example follows in Figure 10.14.

Once again, as you can see on the chart in Figure 10.14, the buying pressure continued after LinkedIn (LNKD) gapped up. Upon a break through the high that occurred prior to 10:00 a.m., or at $229.20s in this case, you could enter a long position. Afterward, place a stop-loss order beneath the low that occurred prior to 10:00 a.m., or once again, use a closer stop or smaller lot size should the low exceed you maximum risk limit. As you likely have already surmised, you can apply the 10:00 a.m. rule to trading gaps to the downside as well. To do so, if a stock gaps down and then makes a new low after 10:00 a.m., you would enter a position by selling the stock short. The chart of Twitter (TWTR) in Figure 10.15 shows a gap-and-go entry that is based on a gap down.

Looking at Figure 10.15, it's possible that you might have entered into a long position upon seeing the reversal bars that appeared shortly after the gap down. Even though it didn't work out in this case, such an entry would not have been wrong. Later, the "Gaining an Edge" section discusses leading indicators you can use that might help you avoid a false entry. However, if you use stop-losses, you'd have set a stop and been out as the stock moved against you. Additionally, as I noted earlier, reversal bar failures can be powerful indicators for entering a trade in the opposite direction, which would have worked well in this case as TWTR in Figure 10.15 showed tremendous

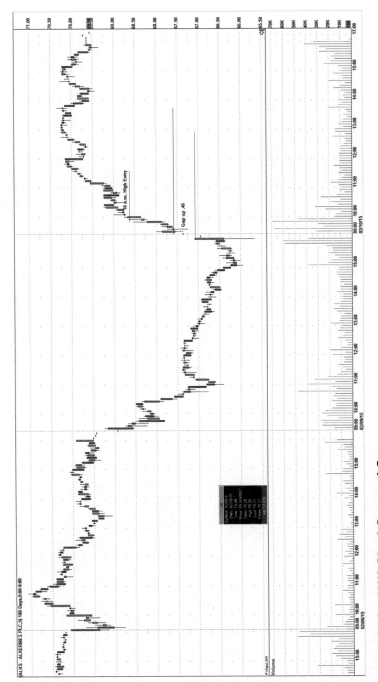

Figure 10.13 ALKS Chart Gap and Go

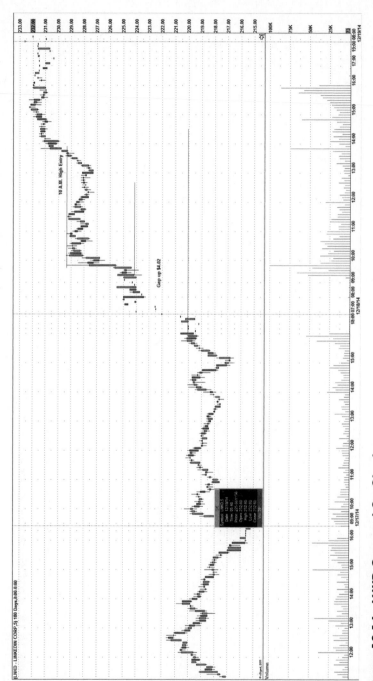

Figure 10.14 LNKD Gap-and-Go Chart

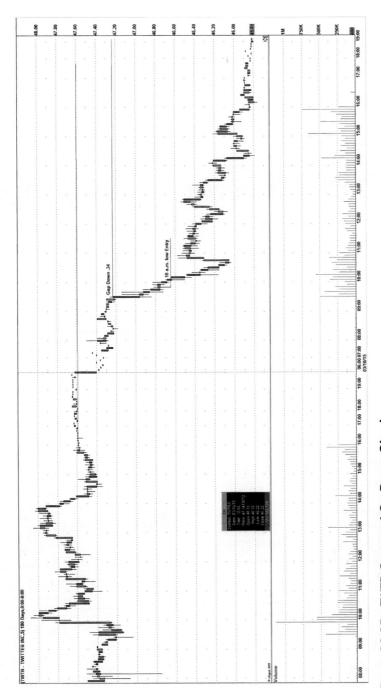

Figure 10.15 TWTR Gap-and-Go Down Chart

151

weakness and broke 10 a.m. lows, thus setting up the killer short at $46.60ish. Regardless of whether you had entered a long position based on the reversal bars, once you stopped out and a breach of the 10:00 a.m. low occurred, you could enter a new position on the short side. Afterward, you would place a stop-loss order slightly above the high that occurred prior to 10:00 a.m. As previously discussed, should such a stop setting be too wide, you can adjust the stop so that it remains within your maximum risk limit (possibly to another nearby area of resistance). The chart of Bank of America (BAC) in Figure 10.16 shows another gap down example. Once again, after BAC gapped down, there was no resulting snapback price reversal. After a brief period of consolidation, the price continued lower.

The low prior to 10:00 a.m. was $16.28. Upon a breach of the $16.27 low, you could sell the stock short, then place a stop-loss order slightly above the high that occurred prior to 10:00 a.m. After entering a gap-and-go trade, you should trail any favorable price movement with your stop-losses, and take profits when appropriate. For more information about these topics, see "Taking Profits" and "Using Stops," later in this chapter. Small gaps or flat opens on days when the market essentially opens flat, or a gap is very small, it's best to wait for the market to establish a directional trend, or bias, before entering a position. Once again, you can use the 10:00 a.m. rule as a guideline. If the market (or your stock) makes a new high after 10:00 a.m., then you would trade it long. Similarly, if it makes a new low after 10:00 a.m., then you would sell it short.

Exit Strategies

Now that you've read about charting techniques to determine gap trade entries, how can you use technical analysis to determine price targets for your exits, and hopefully, exit your trades with a profit? This section explores a few strategies for this purpose. Of course, even though you can use charts to plan your exits, keep in mind that various other overriding factors can also influence, or even dictate, how you exit a gap trade. Your initial objectives for a trade, your expectations, and your daily trading goal can all play a role. Other factors include the individual price action of the stocks you are trading, the behavior of the overall market, and the method you choose for taking profits. For longer trades, the 10:00 a.m. rule

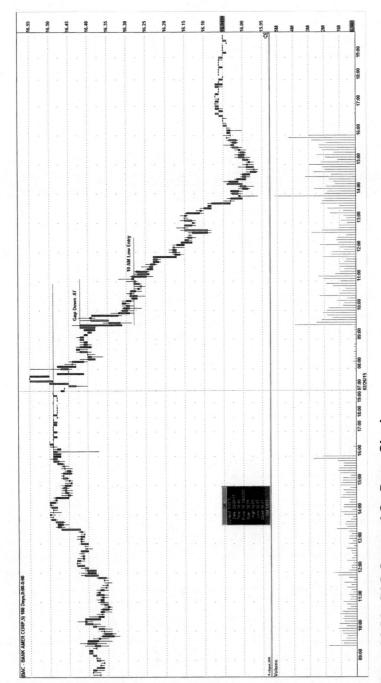

Figure 10.16 BAC Gap-and-Go Down Chart

discussed in this chapter comes into play. Of course, as I mentioned earlier, if the trade goes against you, your exit may be determined by where you place your stop-loss order, or in the case of trailing stop-loss orders, at the point where the price reverses and hits your stop. If you desire to use technical indicators, there are various chart formations you can potentially use for exiting trades, and/or as warning signs where more caution should be exercised. Following, I'll discuss various techniques that I've used to set price targets for exiting my positions and taking profits. I'll also provide examples of technical signals, or warning signs, you can watch for that might indicate a move is losing momentum or about to change directions.

An important area of support or resistance, depending on whether the gap is up or down, tends to occur when a gap fills. That is, when the price approaches the pre-gap price. Generally, this is the prior day's closing price. Therefore, a gap fill is a price target where you should consider taking all or a portion of your profits, or depending on the size of the gap and your gains; you should at least move your stop to break even on the trade. And, since gap fills are widely known as a potential points of resistance (or support, depending on the direction) by other traders, as a gap fill approaches, you may want to act a bit early rather than wait for a complete fill of the gap. If a gap is large and the gap fills, I will definitely take a portion, or all, of my profits. If a more modest gap fills (e.g., a gap of $0.40 or so), depending on how strong the trade appears, I may move my stop to break even, or I may take a portion of my profits and move my stop to break even on my remaining shares. Regardless, I will not allow the trade to turn into a loser at this point. The Microsoft (MSFT) chart in Figure 10.17 shows how resistance is encountered, if only temporarily in this case, after a gap down is filled.

A clean break through the resistance could lead to a continuation of the upside move, which is what subsequently occurred. MSFT as shown in Figure 10.17 hit the gap fill around $41.03 and once it busted through intraday resistance it continued higher. A useful tidbit to note and tuck away for future consideration is that old resistance often becomes an area of new support. Looking at the chart, you can see that once the price broke through the resistance, the old resistance became a new level of support for a period of time.

Other warning signs to watch for are candlestick reversal bars. See "Reversal Bars" at the beginning of this chapter for a general description of the reversal bars discussed here. Candlestick reversal bars

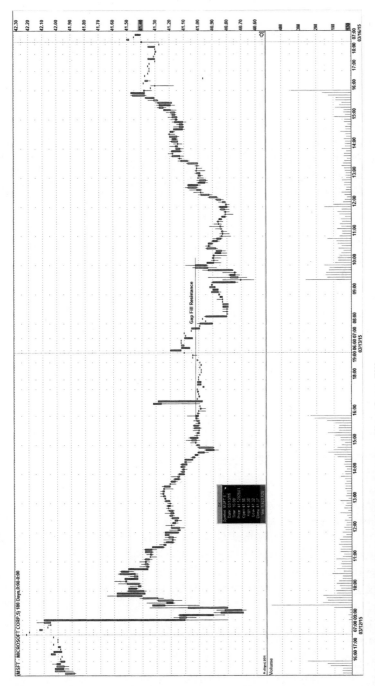

Figure 10.17 MSFT Chart at Resistance after Gap Fill

often appear when a move is running out of steam. For an example of this, look at the MSFT chart in Figure 10.17 and the closeup view of the reversal bars in Figure 10.18. Notice that shortly after the reversal bars appeared, the drive to the upside lost momentum and the price pulled back. The first reversal bar, or candle, in the chart in Figure 10.17 is called a doji. It should be considered a red flag since the price opened and closed within a very tight range. The second candle is called a shooting star (or inverted hammer). One or more of these reversal bars frequently precede uptrend reversals, as they did in this case. Reversal bars are well-known candlestick patterns that are used in technical analysis. Although it's beyond the scope of this book to cover in-depth candlestick charting and the large variety of possible candle formations, if you would like to explore candlestick charting further, there are many good books devoted entirely to the topic. You can visit www.AffinityTrading.com for our current recommendations. Reversal bars can signal the end of a downtrend as well. For an example, see the chart in Figure 10.18 that shows a gap up of Broadcom (BRCM).

Looking at the chart in Figure 10.18, after BRCM gapped up and sold off, you can see that a hammer reversal bar appeared just before the price bounced. A hammer often marks the end of a downtrend. Though I don't always exit a position based solely on the appearance of reversal bars, I do consider reversal bars to be red flags. After seeing one, depending on the situation, I may take a portion of my gains off the table and watch the trade more closely, tighten my stops, or close out a position entirely.

Taking Profits

In previous chapters I discussed the importance of taking profits. Since taking profits applies to all exit strategies when gains are involved, including technical analysis strategies, I'm providing additional comments here that take into account the technical indicators discussed in this chapter. In general, once a price target for your exit has been reached, it's important to be disciplined and take at least a portion of your profits. Your stop should then be moved to breakeven or better on your remaining shares. At this point, under no circumstances should you allow a winning trade to turn into a losing trade. Doing so not only erodes your trading capital, it can be psychologically devastating as well. Therefore, you should consider it a key rule

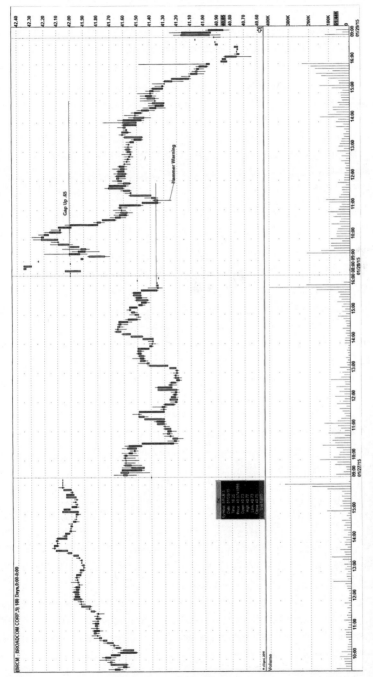

Figure 10.18 Gap Up Chart of BRCM

that must be enforced. Do not allow winners to turn into losers! As I discussed previously, I like to take profits as the trade moves in my favor. I will generally take some money off the table as the price nears the first point of resistance, which is typically the point where the gap fills. However, if I have substantial gains, I may take profits even sooner. Why take the chance of giving it back? Of course, the size of the gap and the amount of gains impact my decisions as well, so this is simply a general guideline that doesn't apply exactly the same to every situation. What I usually do is take profits on half of my shares by the time the gap fills. Depending on how strong the play appears, or how weak, I may even take profits on all of my position. However, if I feel strongly there is more upside, I will sell half of my shares and move my stop-loss order to at least breakeven on my remaining shares (including commissions), or slightly better than breakeven when the situation permits it. I will sometimes tighten my trailing stop at that point as well. For example, suppose I initially have a $0.75 trailing stop. After selling half of my shares, I may tighten my stop to $0.30 or $0.40. If I achieve significant gains on my remaining shares, I'll either take profits on the rest of my shares or I may once again sell half of my remaining shares and continue to trail the move until I stop out of the trade. However, if I see any reversal bars, I will likely take profits right away, or at the very least, tighten my stops.

Obviously, there are many potential variations for how you can take profits, especially when taking your own tolerance for risk into consideration. Many traders take all of their profits at once whenever they have any significant gains, or as a gap fills. My preference is to take money off of the table a piece at a time as I achieve gains, but you can take whichever approach works best for you. The most important point is that you must take profits! Otherwise, you risk giving back all of your gains. Don't beat yourself up if you could have had more gains by staying in a trade longer. It could just as easily have gone against you. If you made money on the trade—you did good! You've likely heard the familiar adage, no one ever goes broke taking profits. This applies to trading gaps as well. Similarly, no one ever picks perfect tops and bottoms, either. If you executed the trade according to your plan, you either made money or got stopped out and preserved your capital, so don't beat yourself up over it. Learn whatever you can from the experience; change your plan, if applicable, and then move on to the next trade.

Know When to Fold 'Em

This section discusses some specific approaches you can consider for setting stop-loss orders. However, as always, you should limit any loss to the maximum you are willing to accept according to your own tolerance for risk. As I've mentioned elsewhere about trading gaps, since gaps tend to be more volatile, I generally use slightly wider stop-loss settings than I might use for other types of trades. Still, the precise setting is subjective and dependent on a variety of factors related to a specific trade. Therefore, you can consider the recommendations here general guidelines, then make adjustments according to the specific circumstances and your own risk limits.

Initial Stop

When planning a gap trade, I typically have a predetermined maximum stop-loss limit in mind for the trade. As market valuations, volatility, gap sizes, and sentiments change over time, I make adjustments to my initial stop-loss settings accordingly. Of course, I make allowances for the size of a specific gap, and the stock's price and historical trading range as well. For example, I would obviously use wider stops for a stock that is trading at $50.00 than I would use for one that is trading at $2.00. Generally, a higher-priced stock will have a larger trading range. It may move $2.00 or $3.00 or more during a day, whereas a $2.00 stock might only move $0.05, $0.10, or $0.20. So, you obviously need to take these factors into consideration when placing your stop-loss orders. If a stock is gapping by $0.50 or $0.60, I might use something like $0.40 or $0.50 for an initial maximum stop-loss limit. For example, if stock XYZ is gapping up by $0.50 and I enter the trade at $50.30, I might place a stop at $49.90 ($50.30 − $0.40 = $49.90).

One psychological area that support or resistance is frequently encountered, if only temporarily, is at round dollar amounts such as $10, $25, $50 or $100. With that in mind, if it's within an appropriate range for a stop, I will often set my stop slightly beneath nearby round dollar amounts. For smaller (or larger) gaps, I would adjust my stop setting accordingly, within reason. Meaning, I don't want to arbitrarily set it too tight, or too large. I might use up to a maximum of about $1 for higher priced stocks that have gapped fairly large, but it's not likely that I would allow a gap trade to go against me by much more than $1.00. The best bet is to test and track the stocks you are playing for gaps and see what they trade like over a period of time at the open. Stocks usually have patterns (trends), so you can see what an appropriate stop might be for any given stock. Daily lows and highs are also price targets that I frequently use for setting my initial stop losses. Since prior lows and highs often establish areas of support and resistance, a break of these could mean a gapping stock's price is not reversing as expected, in which case, I would want to stop out of the trade. When using lows and highs, however, if the stop seems too narrow or too wide, then I would make adjustments so that it falls within a more reasonable range.

Other potential levels of technical support and resistance you might consider for stop-loss settings are gap fills, Fibonacci grid points, or key moving averages. Some key moving averages to keep an eye on for this purpose are the 10-, 20-, 50-, and 200-day moving averages. If you use technical areas of support and resistance for your stop settings, in most cases, it's best to place the stop slightly beyond (or wider than) the desired price target since they are frequently exceeded slightly before holding. A technical area of support or resistance could be a useful alternative when a stop-loss setting based on the approaches described earlier is either too tight, or too wide. When possible, a setting that is comprised of multiple technical indicators is even better, since it tends to be stronger. For example, a setting that coincides with a recent high, a 200-day moving average, and a gap fill is likely to be stronger than any single indicator.

When using technical analysis to plan your entries, a good general guideline to keep in mind for setting stops relates to a failure of the specific pattern that is used for the entry. In other words, you should stop out of a trade when the price movement causes the chart pattern to fail. Stop losses can also be based on the total amount of money that you are willing to lose on a trade. For example, if the most you are willing to lose on a trade is $500 and your lot size will be 1,000 shares, then your maximum stop-loss setting shouldn't be more than $0.50 from your entry price ($500/$1,000 shares = $0.50). Of course, you must also consider what makes sense for a specific trade based on the total purchase price and percentage loss. For example, you wouldn't want to buy 1,000 shares of a $1.00 stock for a total cost of $1,000 and still use $500 as your maximum loss, or a $0.50 stop-loss setting. You would lose $500, or half of your money, before you stopped out of the trade! Of course, this example is only for illustration purposes. As a general rule, we don't play stocks that are under $10.00 for gap trades. I've found that stocks under $10.00 usually don't trade consistently using this technique (or most techniques). The higher the stock price, the more consistent the gaps is a general rule of thumb. Higher-priced stocks tend to be the most volatile as well. Don't be afraid to trade 100 shares of a $70.00 stock as opposed to more shares of a $7.00 stock. Frankly, more often than not, you'll find that you get more bang for your buck with the $70.00 stock!

Using Stops

As time passes or when there is any significant movement in your stock's price, you need to adjust your stop-loss setting. At the very least, the first review of your initial stop-loss setting should occur at 10:00 a.m. At this time, you can use the 10:00 a.m. rule as a guideline for determining where to place your stop. Although the 10:00 a.m. rule is covered elsewhere in the book, for your convenience, here is what it says. If a stock gaps up, you should not buy it long unless it makes a new high after 10:00 a.m. Conversely, if a stock gaps down, you should not sell it short unless it makes a new low after 10:00 a.m. To use the 10:00 a.m. rule as a guideline, adjust your stops to the lows, or highs as the case may be, that were put in prior to 10:00 a.m. For example, if the market gaps down and you enter a long position, when 10:00 a.m. comes move your stop-loss setting for the stock to, or slightly beneath, the low that occurred prior to 10:00 a.m. Conversely, if the market gaps up and you enter a short position, when 10:00 a.m. comes move your stop-loss setting for the stock to the high, or slightly above the high, that occurred prior to 10:00 a.m.

You might be wondering why I'm suggesting that you use the 10:00 a.m. rule for stop-loss placement. The main reason has to do with the way market makers and specialists manage order flow. As orders begin to come in during pre-market trading when volume is light, there may be a lack of either buyers or sellers on a given day. Market makers and specialists must then make a market by taking the other side of the trades with their own inventory. Since they must make money as well (if they want to retain their jobs), they push prices up or down according to the buy or sell bias. After the market opens, during the first 30 minutes of trading there is a higher degree of uncertainty and fluctuation in the market as market makers readjust their inventories. As a result, the market gaps and is more volatile initially. Then once the market makers clear out their inventory imbalances and have made their money, the true market trend begins to develop for the day according to the actual buyers and sellers in the marketplace. Therefore, it's appropriate to review and reset stop-losses relative to the market's true directional trend.

A trailing stop-loss order is a stop that either automatically trails the price of a stock as it moves or is manually adjusted to trail the price movement. You can use trailing stops to trail the price of your long positions as they move higher, or to trail short positions as they move lower. Many of today's trading platforms provide the capability to place stop-loss orders that trail price movements by a specified amount for you automatically. However, if your broker doesn't provide this feature or if you prefer to have greater control over the process, you can also manually adjust stop-loss orders to trail a stock's price movement.

Here's an example of how an automatic trailing stop-loss order works. Suppose that you enter a long position at $50.00 with a plan to stop out of the trade should it initially go against you by $0.50. You also want to use a trailing stop-loss order, rather than a fixed stop-loss order that doesn't change, so you can immediately capture any gains should the price move in your favor. After entering a position at $50.00, you would place a trailing stop-loss order at $49.50. If the stock's price immediately moves against you and falls to $49.50, you'll stop out of the trade with a $0.50 loss. However, if the price goes up $0.25 before pulling back, your stop-loss setting would automatically go up by $0.25 as well. You would now stop out of the trade with a $0.25 loss, if the price fell to $49.75. Similarly, if the price goes up to $51.00 before pulling back, you would stop out of the trade at $50.50 (the high of $51.00 − $0.50 = $50.50) for a gain of $0.50. As you can see, the stop-loss trails any upside movement of the stock's price, minus $0.50, but the stop-loss price does not fall when the stock's price falls. Of course, you can electively choose to sell and take profits at any point you choose.

In the preceding example, you would have obviously come out further ahead by taking profits closer to $51.00, rather than waiting to be stopped out of the trade. Therefore, it's best to use trailing stops, or any stops for that matter, as a method of limiting risk and protecting gains rather than as your sole strategy for taking profits. An advantage to using an automatically trailing stop-loss order is that it shifts a large portion of the responsibility for managing stop-losses to your trading platform, which can be a big help when managing multiple, quickly moving trades at once. On the other hand, an automatic stop doesn't take into account any unique circumstances that might apply to a trade. For example, there might be occasions when you have achieved significant gains, but for one reason or another, you would like to stay in the trade even if it pulls back by $0.55 or $0.60 rather than strictly enforcing the $0.50 trailing stop you initially placed. For instance, maybe you noticed there is a strong level of support $0.10 below where the trailing stop will trigger. Unless you are paying close attention and quickly adjust your trailing stop or change it to a fixed stop, you will be stopped out of the trade if the price falls sufficiently to trigger the stop.

In the case of fixed stops, you assume all responsibility for making any adjustments after placing the initial stop-loss order. As you achieve gains, you need to manually reset your stop-loss order to the desired price. On some trading platforms, you might need to cancel your existing stop-loss order and place a new order, while other systems let you change an existing order without first canceling it. Since this varies, you'll need to check with your broker for the specifics on the types of features that are supported, but regardless of the specifics, it becomes your responsibility to manually adjust your stop-loss orders to trail any upside movement on your trades. It's really a matter of personal preference regarding which type of stop to use.

When playing gaps, you can start with an initial stop that is fixed as described earlier and adjust the stop as the trade evolves, or you can begin with an automatically trailing stop. Another option is to begin with a fixed stop initially, and then switch to a trailing stop later. Whichever method you choose, at the very least, you should begin trailing your gap trades more closely as the gaps fill, or as they take out the prior lows or highs of the day (and recent prior days). And as previously mentioned, it's a good idea to take a portion of your profit at this time and move your stops to break even on any remaining shares.

Before leaving the topic of stop-loss orders, I'll discuss a question that I frequently receive about which type of stop-loss order is best to use, a stop-limit order or a standard stop-loss order. Some trading platforms don't provide an option to specify stop-limit orders. If your trading platform doesn't offer such an option, then you may have no alternative but to use a standard stop-loss order. Since a standard stop-loss order executes as a market order once triggered, in a fast moving market your order could fill at a price that is worse than your intended stop price. If you want to be certain that your order fills after your stop triggers, then you can't do anything to avoid this potential outcome. While you can use a stop-limit order that fills only if your limit price is met, this could leave you exposed to additional risk. If a rapidly moving price does not precisely hit your limit price (i.e., it jumps over your limit price), your order will not execute. For example, if you place a stop-limit order on a long position with a stop price at $25.35 and a limit price at $25.35, when the stock's price hits or falls below $25.35, your stop will trigger and your order will execute as a regular limit order at $25.35. If the stock's price is moving quickly and falls to $25.36, then to $25.34 or lower without specifically hitting $25.35 (or for whatever reason, the price gaps below your limit price), your stop will trigger but your limit order will not fill. The $25.34 price would be lower than your specified minimum limit of $25.35, which prevents the execution of the limit order. The price could subsequently fall to $22.00 or lower and you will not stop out of the trade. A regular stop-loss order that executes as a market order ensures you will stop out of a trade. Though there is no guarantee your order will fill precisely at the specified stop price, your order will fill.

Practically speaking, when trading liquid stocks, in most instances your order will fill reasonably close to your stop price. On the other hand, with fast-moving, low-volume stocks, you could experience worse fills. Regardless, using the preceding example, I would prefer to stop out at $25.20, or whatever, rather than not stop out at all. Since that's my preference, I use and recommend using a standard stop-loss order that executes as a market order once triggered. As always, though, you should take the specific circumstances of a trade into account. There may be unique situations where a stop-limit order is appropriate, like when holding swing trades overnight, and a gap could take out your stop before you've had a chance to review the situation. This isn't a concern for me because I remove all of my stops before the market closes each day and reset them the following morning, which avoids the possibility of gaps taking out my stops. Another approach you could consider is to set the limit price of a stop-limit order somewhat lower than the stop price to help ensure your order fills, but for general trading purposes, I still prefer to use a standard stop-loss order over a stop-limit order.

Gaining an Edge

Traders are always looking for a way to achieve an extra edge—that is, a way to stay a little ahead of the rest of the crowd. Anything that might provide an early indication of a potential change in a stock's price movement, or the overall direction of the market, could be quite beneficial, and profitable. Leading indicators, or those that tend to lead the market, are one method by which traders can obtain an edge. The futures are one type of leading indicator. They are a great way to get a sense of the market's directional bias, which is one reason you commonly see them displayed on business-oriented news broadcasts. Virtually all professional traders watch the futures. Since the futures are leading indicators, if the futures are roaring higher, or falling off a cliff, then the market is likely to follow. Traders predominately watch the Nasdaq 100 and S&P 500 index futures. Most direct-access brokers provide a way to track the futures. However, the method for doing this can vary between brokers. You can check with your broker for more specific information about how to obtain futures quotes and charts using their trading platform.

The Nasdaq Composite can also be used as a leading indicator for the directional bias of technology stocks. The Nasdaq is comprised predominately of technology stocks, and technology frequently leads the market. Why? Technology is the future and everyone wants to bet on the future rather than the past. So, overall, technology is a leading indicator. Similarly, you can use the Semiconductor Index (SOX) as a leading indicator as well. Computer chips are increasingly being put into a larger variety of products, and this trend is currently expected to continue indefinitely into the future. Therefore, the SOX is also a leading indicator.

When used as tools for directional guidance, you generally don't trade the leading indicators themselves (although, it is possible to trade them using options or futures in some cases). For the intended use discussed here, the idea is to watch leading indicators for an indication of how stocks are likely to move. If you want to use leading indicators such as the $BKX (banking index) or $SOX (semi-conductor index) or the Nasdaq for guidance, you need to watch stocks that tend to move along with the SOX or Nasdaq. A few current examples include technology stocks such as Apple (AAPL),

Intel (INTC), Facebook (FB), and Applied Materials (AMAT). These are only a few examples for illustration purposes, and not specific recommendations. The best stock choices change over time. However, you can simply watch some good candidates for a few days. If you repeatedly observe that whenever the leading indicators you are tracking are going up or down, certain stocks are also up or down, then they are potential trading candidates. In situations where the leading indicators have begun to move, but the corresponding stocks you've identified are lagging the move for no apparent reason (news, etc.), there is a good chance the stocks will play catchup at some point, and as a result, they could provide potential trading opportunities. Chapter 12, "Trading Laggards," discusses topics similar to this as well. Two chart examples shown in Figures 10.19 and 10.20 show the Nasdaq and Dow Jones indexes (DIA).

Referring to Figure 10.19, notice the shooting star reversal candle that not only signaled a potential market reversal and the high of the day, it marked an area of potential future resistance. The next morning, the market gapped through the resistance of the prior high, but then it temporarily paused on a pullback as it encountered support in the same area as the prior resistance. Old resistance frequently becomes an area of future support, even if only temporarily. Also notice that once again, a shooting star reversal bar signaled the reversal that occurred shortly after the gap up. Another key area of support is a 200-day moving average, as well as prior swing point lows. Support tends to be even stronger when more than one indicator is involved. Looking at the chart in Figure 10.20, you can see that support was encountered near these levels. The chart in Figure 10.21 shows how the DIA behaved during the same time period as the Nasdaq chart in Figure 10.19.

Notice the similarities between the two charts. Similar to the Nasdaq, the DIA formed a shooting star reversal bar that also marked the high of the day. After the gap up the next morning, additional reversal bars signaled the subsequent pullback. I've also included a Fibonacci grid on this chart (most good charting software provides the capability to overlay Fibonacci grids). Fibonacci grid lines are widely used in technical analysis to indicate potential areas of support and resistance, or potential price pivot points. Though it is beyond the scope of this book to provide in-depth descriptions of Fibonacci grids, there are many good books on technical analysis that explain their use (you can check www.AffinityTrading.com for

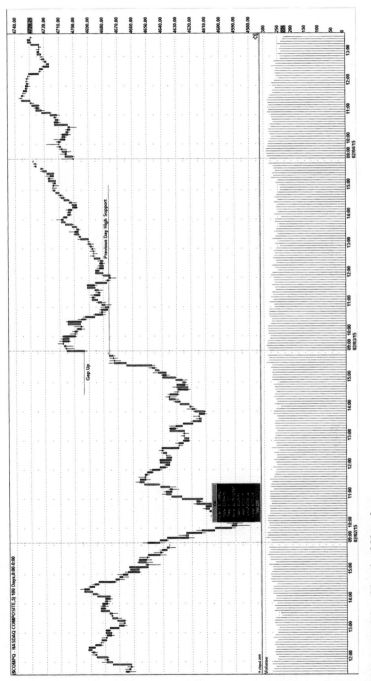

Figure 10.19 Chart of Nasdaq

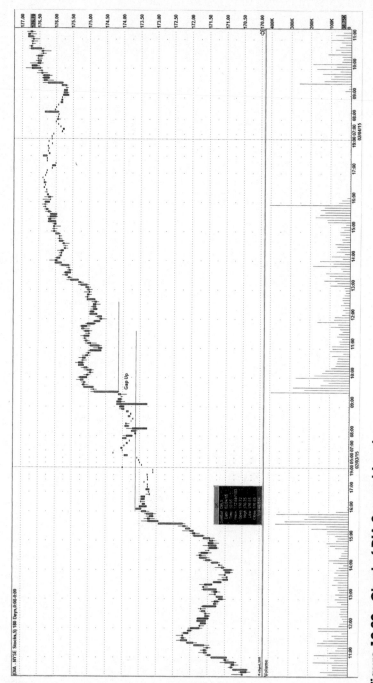

Figure 10.20 Chart of DIA Support Levels

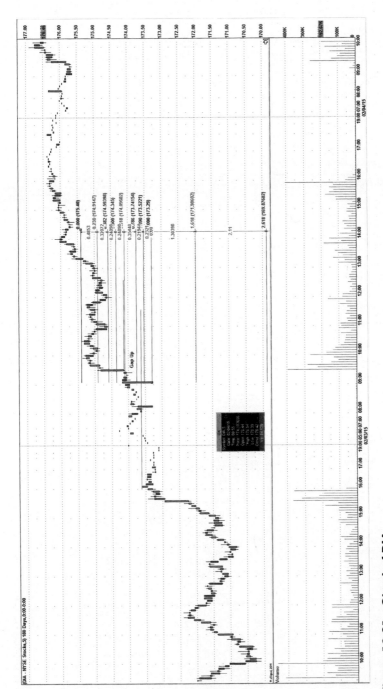

Figure 10.21 Chart of DIA

our latest recommendations). In this case, just note that a level of support was established near the 50 percent Fibonacci grid line, which subsequently held the next day as well. By watching the futures, the Nasdaq composite, and the SOX for reversal signals or areas of support and resistance, you can get an extra edge, or advance warning of what may lie ahead for your stocks. If you see a reversal bar or notice the market is approaching an area of support or resistance, you should at least pay closer attention to your trades. And in some cases, you may even want to consider entering positions, exiting positions, or tightening stop-losses on positions based on what you observe using leading indicators.

CHAPTER

11

News Rules! Trading News

I n today's ever-changing world, where we are fed sometimes second-to-second stimulus, often force-fed to us even if we try to avoid it, through traditional media outlets like TV and radio, but even more so now by social media, we need to have at least a defense prepared for a flash news story. And, it's even better if we have a good offense and can generate winning trade ideas using the *news*.

A vast array and variety of news stories break each day that could potentially impact the stock market or specific stocks. They range from world news events to national news events to news about individual industries or companies.

Laggard News

When we worry about a Grexit (i.e., Greece leaving the European Union) or what the Fed might or might not say is in the air ... when the state of the economy, an earnings announcement or other news impacts the performance of a company, the market often anticipates that other similar companies will be impacted as well. Even though there might not be a sound reason for the news to affect other companies, just the perception that it could may be sufficient to move stock prices. As a result, when positive news comes out about a company that drives its stock price higher, traders and investors may begin looking for other similar stocks they can buy at a cheaper price. Alternatively, the same is true when the news is negative and a stock's price falls. Traders may look at other similar stocks for shorting opportunities.

For example, if a stock in the biotech sector such as Giliad (GILD) releases a huge upside earnings announcement or other positive news, it could be perceived as good news for other stocks in the biotech sector.

If you knew that the price of another biotech stock such as Celgene (CELG) and the price of GILD tended to move together, you could watch CELG for a possible trading opportunity.

Eventually, the linkage between some popular momentum stocks may become so pervasive that the prices may move in sync with one another without a specific reason. If the price of one moves, particularly if it is a significant move, then traders that are familiar with its competitors start watching them for potential trading opportunities. Chapter 12 provides more information about this type of behavior as well.

By having a historical perspective about how a given type of news has affected individual stocks or the overall market in the past, and whether other similar stocks were also affected, you can potentially profit from trading the news. This chapter discusses issues related to trading the news and provides examples of how various types of news releases impacted the market or individual stocks.

Guidelines for Trading News

When trading the news, there are two overriding factors that go into my decision making.

- The overall condition of the market
- The historical context of the news

Market Conditions

I always take current market conditions into account when deciding whether, or how, to make trades that are based on breaking news events. Generally, but depending on the specific circumstances, I prefer not to fight the *direction* of the market and, possibly more important, I don't want to fight the psychology or *perceptions* of the market. If positive news comes out about a company but the market is in a strong downtrend, I am less likely to trade the news. Alternatively, if the news is positive and the market is also posturing positive and in an uptrend, I would be more inclined to trade the news by entering a long position. From March 2009 through at least the beginning of 2015 when I am writing this book, with very few interruptions, the market has been a buy on every, any, and all *dips*. So, clearly during this time frame, you'd be better off playing from a positive bent. When that changes, and it will (markets, like life, are always evolving), then playing the news will involve knowing how the market is trading overall.

Of course, there are always lulls during any particular day, or over a short period of time, so the same can apply to negative news. If the market appears weak and the news is negative, then I would be more likely to trade the news by entering a short position.

However, market psychology is equally as important and may even override the preceding market trend considerations in some circumstances. If the market has little tolerance for a particular type of negative news, then the impact on a stock's price will likely be more dramatic. In situations such as this, the price of an individual stock could easily move contrary to the direction of the market.

The potential for the market or individual stocks to react differently to similar news events at a given point in time is the reason you not only need to have a historical perspective, which is discussed in more detail next, you also need to be in tune with the current mood of the market.

The best trading opportunities often come about when various factors reinforce and align with one another, that is, when positive news comes out about a company while the market is in an uptrend, and the market sentiment related to the news has also been positive. The same applies when all of these factors reinforce one another in a negative way.

Historical Context of News

As mentioned, an important aspect of trading breaking news is having a historical context in which to consider the impact of the news. You need to know how a particular type of news has affected other stocks that have had similar news, and preferably, how it affected their competitors, their sector, or the market at large. With a frame of reference that puts the news into a proper context, you'll be in a position to determine whether the affected stocks or their competitors are good trading candidates.

Since a historical perspective is desirable, it's a good idea to watch breaking news over a period of time and study how it affects individual stocks, sectors, and the market overall before putting your capital at risk. In time, you can develop a historical perspective to help guide your trades.

The significance of the news is also an important consideration. The bigger the news, the better because major news events result in more volatility and larger price swings, which in turn provides better trading opportunities.

Following are some examples of breaking news events and how they impacted the performance of individual stocks and/or the market overall.

News Stories

As previously mentioned, the effect of breaking news is subject to overall market conditions and market psychology. Just because breaking news has a certain effect at one point in time doesn't necessarily mean it will have exactly the same effect at a later time. Market reactions to a particular type of news often change over time.

Old Hat

In the case of extensive ongoing news coverage, news may become *old hat* over a period of time. When it becomes *old news,* the impact it has on the performance of stocks may diminish. In fact, this trends to be one of the safest and best trading setups I've experienced over my 15+ years of trading. Therefore, when reviewing the following examples, remember to take current market conditions into consideration. Also, keep in mind that these examples are simply a random sampling among many other possible news stories that could have an effect on a stock or the overall market.

Stock Spin-Off by Company

While this type of news doesn't happen often, you can see by the reaction of FCAU that when it does the reaction can be very powerful. FCAU announced that it was spinning off Ferrari, and clearly the market liked the news (see Figure 11.1)!

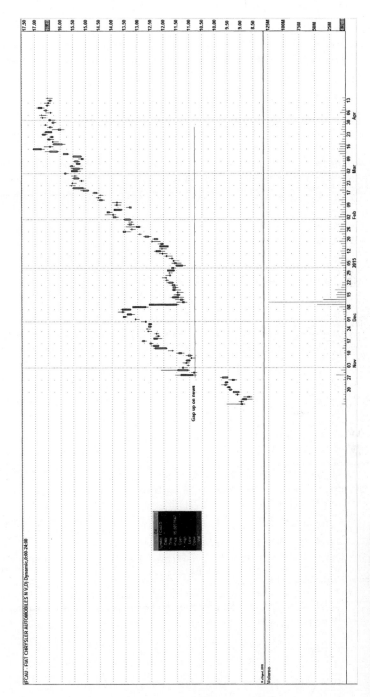

Figure 11.1 Chart of FCAU

Another example of this is when EBAY (see Figure 11.2) announced it was spinning off PayPal. Again, you can see the stock had a tremendously positive reaction to this news initially.

This is a very strong trend, but in reality the real play is not the initial pop, but rather the *spin-off trend*, which I discuss in Chapter 13.

Insider Trading (MSO)

Some news is timeless and has 100 percent correlation, or something close to it. News related to insider trading can also impact the performance of a stock. Following is a news report that came out about Martha Stewart Living Omnimedia, Inc. (MSO) years ago. Some of you may remember this from the *New York Times* on June 7, 2002:

> The *New York Times* reports that Martha Stewart, CEO of MSO and a close friend of the former CEO of IMCL, sold all her shares in IMCL a day or two before the co announced an unfavorable ruling by the FDA, according to people close to a Congressional Investigation of the co. The House Energy and Commerce Committee is Investigating IMCL and has asked for information on which relatives and friends of former IMCL CEO Dr. Waksal had sold shares in the days before the FDA decision.

Figure 11.3 is a chart of MSO that shows the stock's reaction to the news. Once again, this news came out at a time when the market had a low tolerance for company scandals. There had been a string of large companies whose top management was under investigation for illegal accounting practices, insider trading, fraud, and more. Making matters worse, MSO is a unique situation where the company's image, its name, and the brand of its products are all tied to the credibility and prestige of a single individual, the CEO of the company. The company's name is the CEO's name, and the CEO's name is on the company's products. Therefore, if the CEO's reputation is questioned, it has a greater likelihood of adversely impacting the company's sales and its stock price. Even though many analysts were coming out in defense of both the stock and the CEO, I felt the stock couldn't possibly hold up in the face of such news, particularly when the company's name and its product brands are so closely tied to the reputation of its CEO. I also knew how the market had been reacting to this type of news. So, I decided to trade the stock and

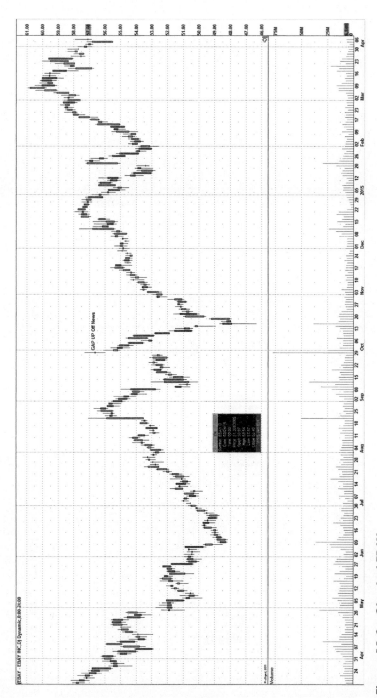

Figure 11.2 Chart of EBAY

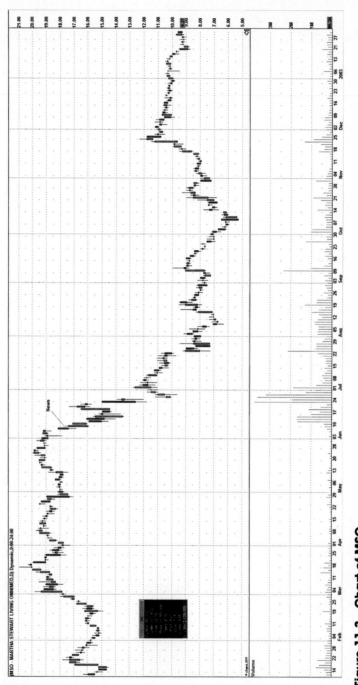

Figure 11.3 Chart of MSO

called it as a short trade for my clients, betting the price would fall, which it subsequently did as can be seen in Figure 11.3. This was a situation that I felt justified a longer-term swing trade, so we bought *put* options on the stock. However, taking a short position would have worked as well. I chose *put* options in part so we could trade the stock with a predefined maximum loss.

Absurdly Cheap News (THC)

Sometimes a stock is so cheap, and it's been beaten down so much, that nearly anything will send the stock into a short squeeze situation. Another blast from the past was The Tenet Healthcare Corp (THC) stock that had been beaten down severely when the following *Barron's* news came out on November 18, 2002:

> Tenet Healthcare "absurdly cheap." Delta Partners manager Charles Jobson has been averaging down in Tenet. The hedge fund manager, whose fund is up 25.5% this year, began buying THC when it first broke $28 and has been buying it more aggressively at $14–$15. "However bad it can get, it can't get as bad as the decline in the share price suggests. The stock is absurdly cheap." Jobson is also bullish on PacifiCare (PHSY) as a turnaround play.

Figure 11.4 shows how the THC stock reacted to the news.

There was considerable short interest in the THC stock due to prior bad news. Therefore, any good news could potentially trigger buying that results in a short squeeze and strong upside price movement. As always, you want to consider the risk/reward potential for a trade. Does the news reflect a real or perceived change in the value of the company? On a short-term basis for that particular day, it did, so the overall risk/reward was favorable for a trade. Once again, I wasn't interested in taking a long-term position in the stock. I was only interested in whether it could be traded for a profit intraday. Even though this news wasn't phenomenal, since the stock was so heavily beaten down and heavily shorted, the news was sufficiently positive for a profitable intraday trade.

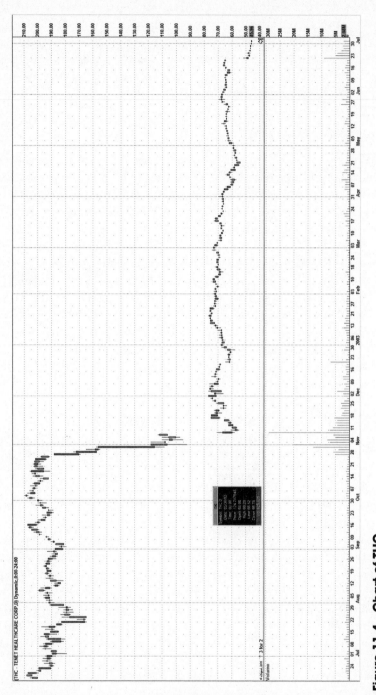

Figure 11.4   Chart of THC

Earnings Guidance (TWTR)

Earnings announcements may also provide trading opportunities. Here is an earnings-guidance news release for Twitter (TWTR), courtesy of Zacks from October 28, 2014:

> Shares of Twitter, Inc. (TWTR) slumped 9.8 percent a day after the company reported a sequential drop in addition of monthly active users in the third quarter. Twitter's fourth quarter revenue projection was also less than analysts' expectations.

Figure 11.5 shows how TWTR reacted to the news.

Even though the preceding news wasn't particularly positive, and the stock sold off after hours initially, the stock didn't ultimately sell off as a result of the news. Instead, the stock gapped up and kept on going. Why? The news appears to be bad! This is a classic case of "sell the rumor–buy the news." The problems related to this news were well known in advance, and the stock had been selling off in the days prior to this news release. Once the news was finally released, there was a relief rally and the stock traded higher. Most everyone expected TWTR's MAUs to be flat to down, so the news was already priced in. The bad news happened as everyone expected, there were no more sellers, and the stock actually moved very strongly the next day, from an after-hours low of around $36 to an intraday high the next day around $49! That's one helluva swing if you can catch it! We sent an alert to buy TWTR on any after-hour dip, expecting what happened to happen. It doesn't always work, but when it does—*Yowsa!*

The way the news is presented also contributes to a more optimistic perception. It was pointed out that the news had been "well-advertised" in advance and "fell within the range of expectations," and even though the guidance was presented as "somewhat" of a surprise, the overall tone of the news report was positive. This, combined with the fact the stock had already sold off heavily ahead of the news, resulted in the relief rally rather than more selling. Had the news been presented with a negative connotation, the stock might have sold off on the news. I provided this example primarily to illustrate how market psychology and perceptions come into play. You need to know how the market and individual stocks have recently reacted to a given type of news, and also take into consideration whether the spin on the news is positive or negative. Plus, you should take into consideration the stock's price action leading up

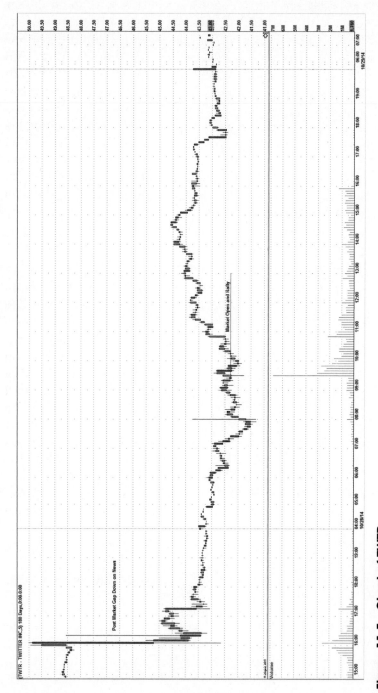

Figure 11.5 Chart of TWTR

to the news, and whether it correlates to prior news about the same subject matter, that is, whether it is "old" news or "new" news.

The time frame is also an important consideration. The same news might have resulted in a selloff three months earlier. Under different market conditions, companies may sell off even when they give upside earnings guidance, so you want to base your decisions on relatively recent market conditions and reactions to recent news. In this case, since the initial gap up was so large, it might have been difficult to enter a long position. However, you would have at least known not to short the news, just because it seemed bad, as many traders might have done. If you take all of the issues discussed above into consideration, you are less likely to find yourself on the wrong side of a news-related trade.

Rumors

A lot of traders play rumors, and I occasionally play rumors as well. The idea is to find an edge, so if I think it will make my clients money, I'll play almost anything. However, it has to be a rumor that is based in reality and something that I feel other traders might pick up on, which could potentially drive the price action. If there's just a rumor on Joe Blow's website that Tim Cook, AAPL's illustrious CEO, is going to step down, then I'm not going to play it. It's not likely Tim Cook is going to step down based on a rumor put out by Joe Blow. On the other hand, if it's a rumor coming from a credible service from which we've had good success in the past playing rumors, then I might play it. If Tim Cook was really stepping down, after guiding AAPL from the mid-$300s to $700s during his tenure, then *that* would be a huge negative to AAPL stock, more than likely.

Of course, a rumor needs to be playable. For example, virtually every week you hear rumors that this company or that one is going to buy out some other company. In most cases, these types of rumors result from someone posting them on websites simply to try and get a stock moving.

A rumor needs to be reasonably credible and based in reality. Otherwise, I just don't play it.

Potential News

I have a pretty hard-and-fast rule—don't play *potential* news. The best example of this is that many traders like to *gamble* on what a

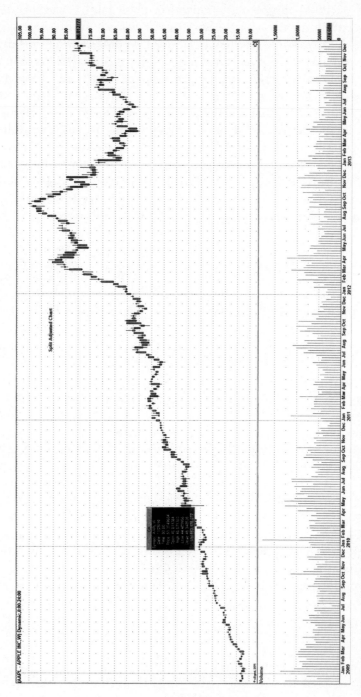

Figure 11.6 Chart of APPL during Tim Cook's Tenure

company will do post-earnings report. They take *shots* often with options, thinking they have some sort of (often-misguided) edge. They thought TWTR would have a bad report, they were right, but the stock went *up* instead. Or, they thought another company might have a great report, but the stock went down. Earnings often produce wild swings in a company's stock. I try to avoid guessing which way the stock will swing post-earnings. Have I ever held into earnings? Yes, and my record is pretty good overall, but when I do, it is usually based on some other factors, like what other stocks in the same sector have done following their earnings. I try to have some *real* edge, rather than some perceived edge. Just remember, *hubris* is not a good trading psychology. The minute you think you have something figured out and it "can't lose" is the minute you are likely to blow up your account—better to be safe than sorry!

In my opinion, it isn't worth the risk. The play is to sell before the earnings report comes out. That is the trend!

Managing Risk

You should always consider the risk exposure from unexpected news events, and not overexpose yourself with too many earnings plays at once.

Actually, that applies to trading any trend. Even though the earnings trend is a powerful trend, unexpected major news events like the September 11, 2001, terrorist attacks can take the market and your stocks down regardless of the strength of a trend. The same is true of individual stock news. If a company announces it is going out of business two days ahead of earnings, the stock price isn't likely to go up. Therefore, you should only use a portion of your total funds to trade any single trend. Similar to the window-dressing trend (see Chapter 13 for more), earnings plays are nice because, once again, you have defined risk over a relatively short time frame. You define and limit your risk two ways, by using a stop-loss order to define your monetary risk and by controlling the length of time you are in the trade.

To reduce your time-based risk exposure further, you can wait until the earnings report is closer before entering a trade. And as with any trade, upon entering a position you should immediately place a stop-loss order according to your own risk tolerances to guard against excessive monetary losses should the trade go against you for any reason.

12

Trading Laggards

Even though the lion has no spots, and the leopard can't change his or hers—they are both still cats at heart. They are different but they often display similar characteristics. The same goes for stocks. The prices of stocks that are in a similar business, industry, or sector will often move together. When the price of one goes up or down, the price of other similar stocks may go up or down as well. For example, if you look at their charts, you'll see that the price actions of two closely related biotech stocks, such as Amgen (AMGN) and Biogen-Idec (BIIB), often move together. One of the best examples no longer exists since both stocks were bought out by Barry Diller's IACI, but we'll use them to prove out the point. These were two travel industry stocks: Expedia (EXPE) and Hotels.com (ROOM). They were known to move so closely that a good trader could often catch $2 to $3 moves by following them and using the laggard techniques we'll be discussing in this chapter.

What Is a Laggard?

When a stock's price action is lagging behind its peer stocks, which are stocks in a comparable business, industry, or sector, it is called a laggard. A price divergence between a laggard and a peer stock frequently corrects itself at some point, either intraday or within the next day or so. The price action of a laggard often catches up with the price action of a peer stock, but this is also subject to the specific circumstances, news, or overall market conditions. In some instances, the price of the peer stock will move back toward the price of the

laggard. To help judge which stock is most likely to make a corrective move, you can look at the strength and direction of the overall
market. If the market is moving higher and a laggard's peer stock
is moving higher, the lagging stock is likely to also move higher to
catch up. Conversely, if the market is moving lower and a laggard's
peer stock is moving lower, the lagging stock is also likely to eventually
move lower.

If It Looks Like a Laggard, and It Smells Like One ...

Laggards can provide great intraday trading opportunities. For
example, maybe the biotech sector starts getting attention. You
could start watching some biotech stocks that tend to move together.
Once again, I'll use AMGN and BIIB as an example, but this could
apply to other stocks as well. Suppose you notice that AMGN is up $2
but BIIB is essentially flat. Since BIIB is lagging behind the AMGN
move, unless there is some type of bad news out about BIIB, which
you should check, BIIB may eventually take off and catch up with
AMGN. Therefore, you might look to buy BIIB long for a trade.
There are many intraday trading opportunities such as these. If you
identify and watch stocks that tend to run together, you can watch
for intraday price divergences between them.

Watchlists

One of the most underrated trading tools that any type of trader can
make ample use of, and easily set up, is a *watchlist.*
     If you trade on a platform that doesn't allow you to have a
watchlist—well, I strongly suggest you trade elsewhere. You can also
use the watchlist feature *for free* at www.worldseriesoftrading.com.
There is also a great charting software for free there as well.
     You can set your watchlist up simply by segregating sectors so that
there is some logic to it. Don't get sloppy here, as you'll miss potentially valuable winning trades if you do!

Sectors

I like to set up my watchlist starting with sectors I generally trade, or
trade more often than others. So, for example, I trade *tech* a lot (see
Tech Watchlist), and that is typically at the top of any of my watchlists.

I'd subdivide tech into four groups:

1. Old tech—this includes CSCO, INTC, IBM, MSFT.
2. Internet—this includes GOOG, AAPL, YHOO, EBAY.
3. Social media—this includes FB, TWTR, LNKD, ANGI, GRPN.
4. Internet security—this includes PANW, CYBR, FTNT, FEYE.

I'll add to these starting points as I see a new issue come up that qualifies for a subsector. Or, I'll add because perhaps a stock I don't normally trade has news that makes it tradable. Obviously, if a stock becomes irrelevant, or is one that you can't define laggard or other patterns/trends with, then you can easily remove it from your list.

Tech Watchlist:

QQQ—Nasdaq index
CSCO—Cisco
INTC—Intel
IBM—IBM
MSFT—Microsoft
SNDK—SanDisk
AMAT—Applied Materials
EMC—EMC
BRCD—Brocade
GOOG—Google
GOOGL—Google
AAPL—Apple
YHOO—Yahoo
EBAY—eBay
NFLX—Netflix
PCLN—Priceline
EXPE—Expedia
AMZN—Amazon
BABA—Alibaba
BIDU—Baidu
SINA—Sina

WB—Weibo

TWTR—Twitter

FB—Faccebook

LNKD—Linked In

GRPN—Groupon

GPRO—Go Pro

PANW—Palo Alto Networks

FEYE—Fire Eye

CYBR—Cyber Arc

FTNT—Fortnet

Next, I'll go to *biotech* and start doing the same thing. I'll divide this group into subsectors as well, though oftentimes biotech either goes up or down. There's a herd mentality, unless of course one or more stocks or a particular sector has company- or sector-specific news. Sometimes my watchlist is a few stocks and sometimes it'll be as long as 30 or 40 stocks, depending on market action and if I'm swinging stocks or just playing intraday. Rather than spend an inordinate amount of time and kill more trees than needed, I'll give you the few-stocks example. Obviously this changes over time, but it's easy to set it up to *your* comfort and style.

My Watchlist:

BBH—Biotech Index

AMGN—Amgen

BIIB—Biogen

REGN—Regeneron

ALKS—Alkemites

CELG—Celgene

GERN—Geron

BMY—Bristol Myers

Add any others that are hot or cold at the moment.

Figure 12.1 is another example of two stocks, Expedia (EXPE) and Priceline. com (PCLN), which have similar price action. Both sell hotel and airline reservations online, travel vacations, and other

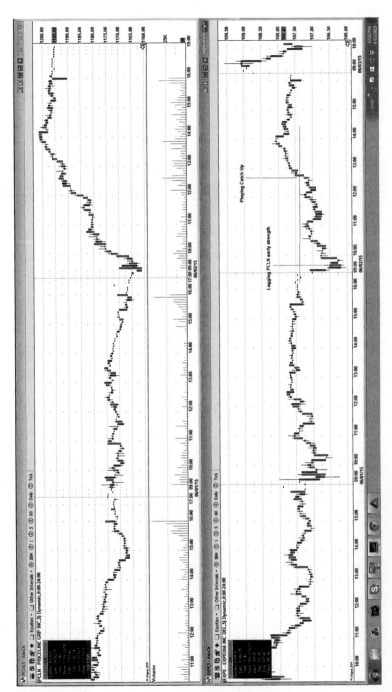

Figure 12.1 Chart of EXPE and PCLN

191

travel services. Since both stocks are in similar online businesses, news or other announcements that affect the price of one frequently affect the price of the other. Take a look at the chart in Figure 12.1. The chart compares the intraday price action of both stocks. Notice how the overall price action of one tends to coincide with the price action of the other.

Notice on the chart that even though PCLN started the day strong and finished even stronger, EXPE started out weak. EXPE began lagging behind PCLN right at the start of the day. As the day moved on and PCLN got stronger, EXPE played catchup and turned positive. You can also see that they then traded nearly lockstep. Sometimes, a laggard may carry over into the next day before catching up. However, since I don't like the additional risk exposure associated with holding a position overnight, I prefer to play laggards intraday and rarely hold them overnight. Laggards make nice trades because they tend to be high-percentage plays with minimal risk. For example, on a stock like EXPE, you can place a relatively tight stop-loss order of about $1 to minimize risk, but the stock could potentially run $2 or $3 on an intraday move, which is a great risk/reward ratio. When the Nasdaq market is really screaming, either of these stocks is a good candidate for a fabulous intraday ride and profit.

Like everything else, trial and error is key to trading successful and finding your own *mojo*. What works for me may or may not work for you. By setting up a good watchlist, you can easily track this trend on a daily basis and follow along as stocks in similar sectors either move in conjunction with or against others that are similar businesses.

News and Laggards

We talked about how news impacts stocks; it also impacts laggards often. If PCLN has exceptional earnings and pops 10 percent, you can almost bet that EXPE is up as well on the news, assuming it doesn't have news that counters PCLN's good news. Remember, as with everything—*news rules!*

CHAPTER 13

Trends Are Your Friends

Trends can be your best friend—or your worst enemy! You may have heard the phrase, "Trends are your friends," but what does it mean? Well, a trend is your friend when you trade in the same direction as the trend. The momentum of a trend can help drive price movement further in your favor. Alternatively, when trading on the opposite side of a trend, it can just as easily propel the price action against you. In this case, the trend is your enemy. Therefore, it is preferable to trade with a trend rather than against it. Your friends have "got your back" most of the time.

What is a trend? Those of you with exposure to the stock market likely know the meaning of the term *trend* as it applies to the direction of price movement. For example, if the general direction of price movement is upward over a period of time, it is called an *up*trend. Conversely, if the price movement is downward, it is called a *down*trend. In addition to uptrends and downtrends, the term *trend* also applies to the historical tendency for certain market behavior, price action, or patterns to repeat.

There are a variety of trends, and some reoccur with more predictability and reliability than others. Trends may be associated with certain events, time periods, perceptions, or other factors. The duration and frequency of trends vary as well. For example, gap trends occur intraday, while earnings trends occur quarterly, and the January effect trend occurs only once a year. As with the ever-changing market, trends also change. New trends appear, and trends that were once reliable may no longer work as well, or may quit working altogether. Some trends may only work for a relatively short period of time while others may endure for years (e.g., "Buy the rumor—sell the news," the January effect, and earnings trends). The reasons for this vary. It may be because too many people learn about a trend so it no longer works reliably, or because market psychology or overall market conditions that are conducive to a trend change.

For example, during the bull market of the late 1990s, the first trend I discovered and built a reputation on was IPO spinoffs. Another IPO-related trend was quiet-period expirations. Both of these trends could be traded with a high degree of reliability. A few years later, due to changing market conditions, IPOs were in short supply and those that did make it to market weren't traded with the same level of excitement and enthusiasm. The market no longer reacted the same way to IPOs (see the next section for more about market psychology). Consequently, trading the parent companies that spun-off IPOs or IPO quiet-period expirations no longer worked reliably. However, proving out that trends can come back into vogue, our clients played Yahoo! (YHOO), and it was my Stock of the Year in 2013 and 2014 because it owned so much Alibaba (BABA) that I felt YHOO had to go much higher, which it did, into BABA's IPO. As I write this book, early to mid-2015, we are in both Fiat Chrysler (FCAU) because it's spinning off Ferarri and eBay because it's spinning off PayPal. Both positions are up huge for clients, and I expect higher prices still in the weeks and months ahead.

Stick with the Trend!

Although trends are not foolproof, trading in harmony with current trends rather than against them provides an additional edge that can result in a higher percentage of winning trades. Many trends are very high percentage plays with great risk/reward ratios! People often ask me what books I read on the stock market. Actually, I haven't read many. It may seem unlikely, but it's true. What I do read are a lot of psychology books. I like to know what people are thinking, and how they are thinking.

The reason why the market exaggerates moves and allows us to make money is because people are always anticipating something. They are either anticipating good news or they are anticipating bad news. For a long time after the 9-11-01 terrorist attacks, the market ran down on terrorist threats. Any time there was a new terrorist threat, the market tanked! People were shell-shocked, for good reason, obviously, but people were expecting the worst! Whenever someone came on CNBC and said there was a terrorist alert, the market sold off, until it finally got to a point where people became immune to it. Finally, the market could go up. The terrorist alerts didn't matter. The mindset of people had changed. They weren't over 9/11—it's not something you get over—but they were desensitized to threats that fortunately didn't occur. They had heard it all before, and they no longer believed in the threats. Therefore, they just discarded them.

Conversely, whenever the market is running up, people are afraid to miss the boat. Though it's obvious the market can't keep going up forever, the bottom line is, people will keep on buying as long as they are afraid that they may have missed the bottom! One of the guidelines I like to use for market sentiment is when CNBC gets bullish. When everybody starts thinking the same thing, that's the time when you want to be more cautious. It's a contrarian indicator. The last guy in the pool is the one that swims with the turd, right? Usually what happens is, when everyone is positive again, that's when we go back down. Everyone is back in the market, so there aren't sufficient numbers of new buyers coming into the market to sustain prices or drive them higher. Anyway, my point is, human psychology is what drives the market and trends.

Yes, there are computerized "buy" and "sell" programs, but human beings initiate them. They aren't initiated by some dog barking, or some parrot squawking, "Buy, buy, buy!" They come from companies run by human beings like you and me. Well, actually, some may be subhumans, but that's another matter. By and large, they are companies run by people who have blood, we think, and it's the people who decide to put in a buy or sell program. Similarly, trends work because enough people, but not too many, learn about them and believe in them. To a large degree, it becomes a self-fulfilling prophecy. The "buy the rumor—sell the news" trend, earnings runs, the use of moving averages as support, and many other trends work because people know about them and believe they will work.

For example, the 200-day moving average is perceived as a very strong level of support. So when a stock's price falls to its 200-day moving average, people start buying the stock, expecting the underlying support. The additional buying causes the price to bounce, which further reinforces the trend. The same process applies to other trends as well. The idea is to stay one step ahead of the market. In the best-case scenario, we can find trends that only a relatively small number of other people have found, since trends historically work when some people, but not everyone, knows about them. Trends tend to stop working once everyone does know about them. Once everyone knows about a trend, they anticipate it and rush in to play the trend, which leaves no more buyers or sellers to propel the trend forward. If a trend quits working, I don't try to play it anymore. When a trend doesn't play out, I want to know why, so I do research to determine if there are any variables that might have affected the trend. If I don't find any and the trend was just a dud, it raises a caution flag but it doesn't necessarily mean a trend is no longer valid. So, I watch the trend the next time. If it's a loser a second time, then I don't play it any longer until subsequent tracking confirms whether the failures were just temporary blips, or whether the trend is no longer valid.

At any rate, I track these types of things, trend behavior, the overall market sentiment, market psychology, and human nature, and I factor them into my trading plan. My goal is to find proven trends and to take advantage of them for the added edge they provide. As previously discussed, trends come and go or change over time with changes in market sentiment. Before trading any trend, it's best to watch it for a period of time to confirm the trend is still valid under current market conditions.

Window Dressing

Window dressing is a strong trend that tends to occur with a high degree of reliability. Since fund managers are required to report their portfolio's makeup at the end of each calendar quarter, as the end of the quarter approaches, they often buy and sell certain stocks to give the appearance they held stocks that performed well throughout the entire quarter. Stocks they currently hold that performed poorly during the quarter may be sold, and stocks they don't own that performed well may be bought. After the quarter ends, and depending on how favorably they view a particular stock, managers may buy back stocks they previously sold, or sell those they previously bought. The buying and selling of stocks for this purpose is called window dressing.

Timing the Trade

You can trade this trend by watching for poorly performing stocks that sell off hard for no apparent reason (i.e., with no other bad news, etc.) during the last 7 to 10 days of the quarter. Once the selling appears to have subsided, you can enter a long position just before the end of the quarter. During the first week of the subsequent quarter, these stocks tend to bounce back as fund managers buy them back, and/or as other people take advantage of the beaten-down prices. Conversely, you can consider entering a short position on stocks that have run up hard near the end of the quarter due to window dressing, since these are likely to pull back once the quarter is over.

Managing Risk

Frequently, this trend applies to entire groups or sectors of stocks, or even the entire market. For example, the biotech or semiconductor stocks may have performed well, or poorly, during a given quarter. In these cases, another way to play the trend is to buy indexes (QQQ, SPY, OEX, etc.) or holders (BBH, SMH, etc.) that correspond to a particular group of stocks. This is a good alternative when you want to further reduce your risk exposure by not trading an individual stock. To define your risk even more, you can consider buying *call* or *put* options as well. One of the nice things about this trend is the relatively short-term time frame that's involved for a trade. You'll know the outcome of the trade within a few days or a week. And since it tends to be a high-percentage trend, by using stop-loss orders to limit and define your overall risk you can make a potentially powerful trade with a great risk/reward ratio.

Window Dressing Examples

The chart of Apple (AAPL) in Figure 13.1 shows an example of window dressing, or a dressup in this case, resulting from a strong quarterly performance.

On the chart, notice how well the stock performed during the quarter. Since it performed so well, fund managers who wanted to show AAPL on their books for the quarter started buying the stock near the end of the quarter, which caused the price to run up further. See the "Mark Up" time period on the chart. The week after the quarter ended, as shown by the "Take Down" time period on the chart, the stock sold off as fund managers who really didn't want to own the stock long term exited their positions, and/or other

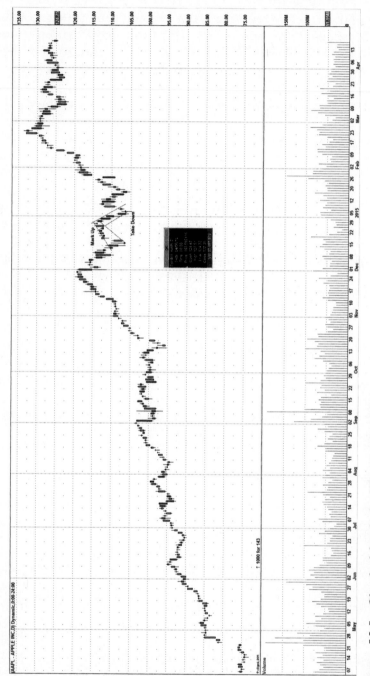

Figure 13.1   Chart of Apple for Window Dressing

profit takers exited positions to take advantage of the excessive runup in price. Figure 13.2 is a chart of Brocade Communication Systems, Inc. (BRCD) that shows another example of window dressing, a dress-down in this case, which resulted from a poor quarterly performance.

Notice on the chart how BRCD performed poorly during the quarter, then sold off further due to window dressing as the quarter ended. See the "Take Down" time period on the chart. During the first week of the next quarter, as shown by the "Mark Up" time period on the chart, the stock bounced back. In this case, fund managers who sold BRCD for window-dressing purposes before the end of the quarter, but still wanted to own the stock longer term, bought the stock back once the new quarter began, and/or other buyers took up positions to take advantage of the beaten-down price. From an investor's point of view, window dressing really isn't in the best interests of those who own the funds. Meaning, managers will often buy back a stock for more than what they sold it a short-time earlier, or conversely, sell a stock for less than what they paid for it. And many times, there are additional commission fees associated with the trades. Regardless, window dressing is a common quarterly practice, or trend, from which traders can potentially profit. We've made many successful window-dressing calls for our clients. As mentioned earlier, this trend often applies to the overall market. In instances where it does, you can use it as an additional indicator of how the market may perform near the end of a quarter, or the beginning of the next quarter. For example, if technology stocks have collectively performed poorly throughout the quarter, the last week of the quarter will frequently be a down week for the Nasdaq market, since many if not most of the larger tech firms are listed there rather than the NYSE.

Earnings Runners

The earnings trend has been a very powerful and reliable trend ever since I began tracking it many years ago. Often, popular momentum stocks will run up 10–20 percent or more ahead of their earnings report each quarter. In most cases, but not always, they will pull back after their earnings report is released, even when the reported earnings are good. It is often a case of "Buy the rumor—sell the news." Sometimes, though, it is like the case of recent IPO (at the time) Shake Shack (SHAK), which sold off around 10 percent at the open the day after earnings, only to stage a *sharp* reversal and go *green*

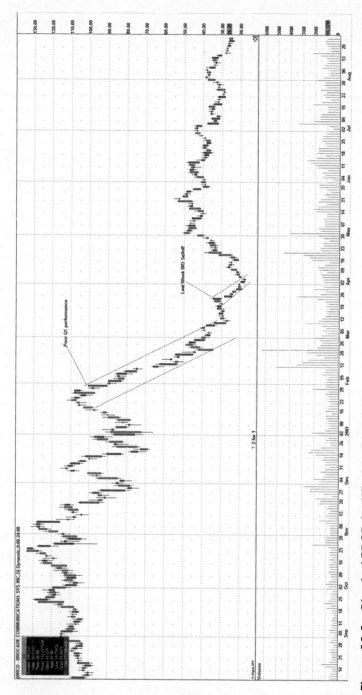

Figure 13.2 Chart of BRCD for Window Dressing

(higher) intraday (see Figure 13.3). That unpredictability is why I prefer to hold into earnings, but not through them. As always, everything is about defining your risk/reward and having a plan. It's hard to have a plan when stocks can open up or down 5, 10, or even 40 percent following earnings.

Timing the Trend

The trend is to buy a stock for a potential run ahead of earnings, generally about 5 to 14 days ahead of its earnings report as you begin to see signs of increased upside interest in the stock, which is indicated by an increase in the stock's price and volume. You sell the stock before the market closes on the day that earnings are reported, or by the end of the prior day when earnings are reported in the morning. In cases where the market is strong, you can consider entering your positions earlier. Conversely, if the market seems weak, you may want to limit your time-based risk exposure by waiting until the earnings report is nearer. I rarely ever hold stocks all the way into their earnings report. Holding a stock into earnings is gambling because there is no way to know what will be reported. If you hold into the earnings and the earnings are worse than expected, you could get crushed.

And as I mentioned earlier, many stocks will sell off after earnings even when the earnings report is good. Repeatedly, I've seen instances where a company blows out earnings and still sells off afterward. There are times when the stock will continue higher after earnings, particularly if a very large upside earnings surprise is reported and the market overall is in a strong uptrend. But since you can't know for certain in advance what the earnings will be, in my opinion, it isn't worth the risk. The play is to sell before the earnings report comes out. That is the trend!

Managing Risk

You should always consider the risk exposure from unexpected news events, and not overexpose yourself with too many earnings plays at once. Actually, that applies to trading any trend. Even though the earnings trend is a powerful trend, unexpected major news events like the 9/11 terrorist attacks can take the market and your stocks down regardless of the strength of a trend. The same is true of individual stock news. If a company announces it is going out of business two days ahead of earnings, the stock price isn't likely to go up.

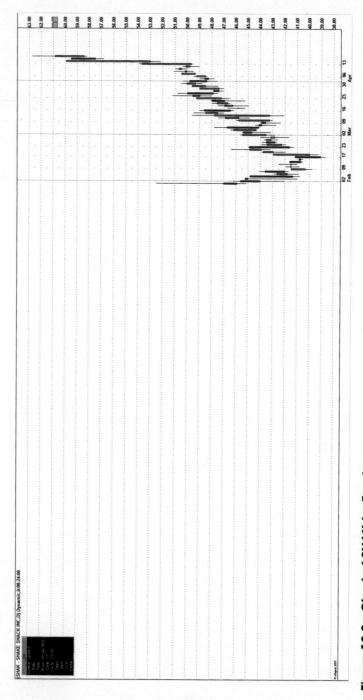

Figure 13.3 Chart of SHAK for Earnings

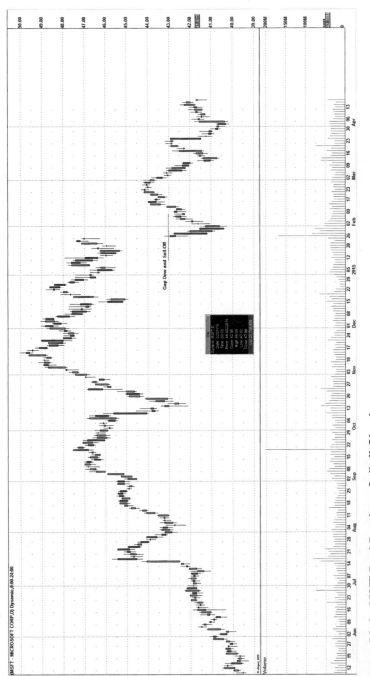

Figure 13.4 MSFT Post-Earnings Selloff Chart

Therefore, you should only use a portion of your total funds to trade any single trend. Similar to the window-dressing trend, earnings plays are nice because, once again, you have defined risk over a relatively short time frame. You define and limit your risk two ways, by using a stop-loss order to define your monetary risk and by controlling the length of time you are in the trade. To reduce your time-based risk exposure further, you can wait until the earnings report is closer before entering a trade. And as with any trade, upon entering a position you should immediately place a stop-loss order according to your own risk tolerances to guard against excessive monetary losses should the trade go against you for any reason. Another way to define your risk is to use *options* to play a trend. Since many of these trends are in effect swing trades, trades where we are holding for a few days or more, and because there is a strong possibility that the stock will move a decent percentage, using options can define your risk and optimize your upside.

The Historical Perspective

Part of trading earnings is becoming familiar with the history of the individual stocks you intend to play. I pick momentum stocks that I know from experience have historically run up ahead of their earnings report. Though I adapt my actual picks to the circumstances each quarter, a few examples of stocks I might watch are AAPL, Facebook (FB), Bank of America (BAC), Amgen (AMGN), and GOOG. However, there are many other stocks that you might also consider, stocks like Adobe (ADBE), BIIB, Goldman Sachs (GS), and AMZN. In most cases, stocks tend to begin a runup ahead of their earnings about one to two weeks out, but this can vary depending on the stock and market conditions. With a historical perspective, you'll be in a better position to time the entries and exits of your individual trades.

Earnings Trend Examples

Figure 13.5 is a chart that shows the price action of FB, an earnings play that we called for members. About one week ahead of earnings you can see the price explosion of FB heading into earnings.

As mentioned earlier, the longer the time until earnings, the greater the risk that bad news or changing market conditions could cause the trade to go against you. So, the precise timing of the entry

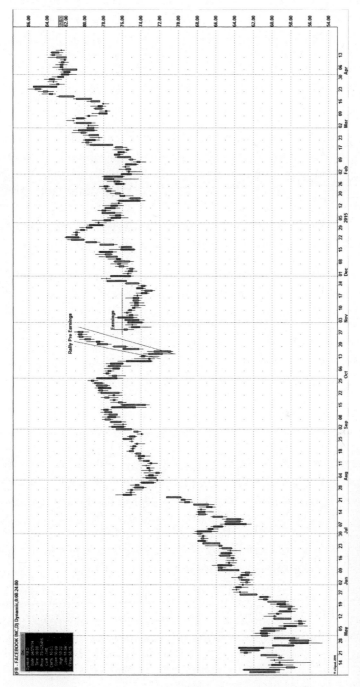

Figure 13.5   Chart of FB into Earnings

depends on your risk tolerance, overall market conditions, and how a given stock has historically traded ahead of its earnings reports. Figure 13.6 is another example that shows the price action of AAPL ahead of its earnings report.

Notice on the chart that AAPL gained about 5 percent in the two weeks prior to reporting earnings. At first glance, that might not seem like much, but for a stock with the market capitalization and volume of AAPL, it is a very large move. The fact that large stocks like FB and AAPL could move so profoundly in a relatively short period of time demonstrates the strength of earnings trends. Since the earnings trends are so powerful, I will frequently trade the big stocks for earnings; however, my preference is to trade other momentum stocks that have a somewhat smaller market capitalization. However, I'm not referring to small, illiquid stocks. The momentum stocks I generally play are still large enough to have substantial market capitalizations and liquidity, as I want to be able to get in and out of trades easily. Some examples of these stocks are SanDisk (SNDK), Twitter (TWTR), LinkedIn (LNKD), Groupon (GRPN), and Intrexon (XON). Momentum stocks that have a smaller market capitalization relative to the largest stocks/companies tend to make larger moves ahead of their earnings reports.

Take a look at the chart in Figure 13.7 that shows the price movement of TWTR ahead of earnings. This is another stock we called for an earnings trade. As you can see on the chart, TWTR had a nice run ahead of earnings. This stock also serves as a good example of why you should always exit your trade prior to the earnings reports. Just take a look at what happened after TWTR reported earnings. The stock gapped down large, so anyone who held the stock through earnings took a major hit. I don't like taking risks where I have no control over the outcome. I don't know whether a stock will blow out earnings or not, so why take the risk? It's best just to exit the trade. If the stock goes up, so what? There will be many other trading opportunities. It's better to manage your risk exposure and preserve capital than gamble on unknown factors out of your control.

FOMC Runs

The FOMC (Federal Open Market Committee) is a 12-member committee that is responsible for setting interest rate and credit policies. Another trend that has been powerful for many years now concerns

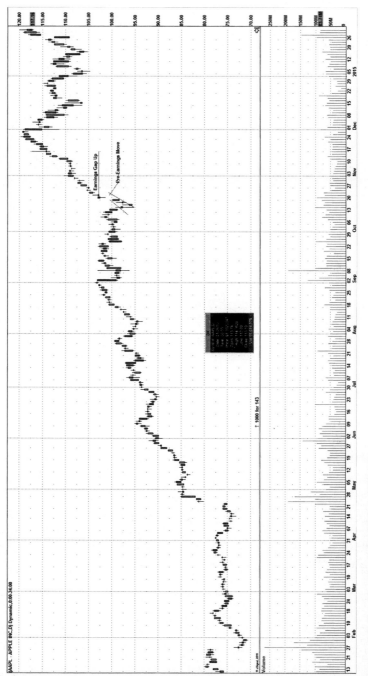

Figure 13.6 Chart of AAPL into Earnings

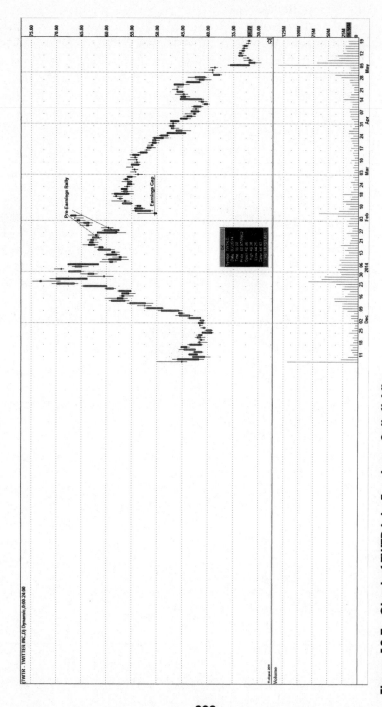

Figure 13.7 Chart of TWTR into Earnings, Selloff After

stock runs and pullbacks surrounding FOMC meetings related to interest rate or other monetary policy announcements—particularly, when people expect an FOMC announcement that will be viewed as beneficial to the market. You can often trade the time before and after FOMC announcements in multiple ways. The dynamics surrounding FOMC meetings are interesting because they are associated with multiple interrelated trends, all of which have the potential to be traded.

Timing the Trade

An FOMC run used to occur one or two weeks ahead of the FOMC, but as I've mentioned many times herein, trends change and we either change with them or get hammered, more often than not. Nowadays, the movement often occurs anywhere from one to seven days out. And on the day of the meeting, you'll frequently see additional intraday trends come into play, which may also be followed by another multiple-day countertrend reaction. Generally, the day of an FOMC meeting tends to be volatile, so once again, you need to take current market conditions into account. What frequently occurs is the market will either run up or down ahead of the meeting, depending on the perceptions of the outcome of the meeting and whether it is positive or negative for the market.

Once an FOMC announcement is made, there is typically a very fast-paced knee-jerk, or impulsive, reaction to the news, which is then immediately followed by another countertrend corrective snapback, and then another reversal back in the direction of the first move, which often follows through until the end of the day. This trend has been virtually 100 percent effective since I began tracking it. I frequently trade the countertrend snapback resulting from the initial impulsive move that follows the FOMC news announcement and the final move in the original direction. I call this fading the first move, or fading the first spike—then fading the fade. Regardless of whether the first impulsive move is to the upside or downside, it tends to fade back in the opposite direction. It is possible to trade all of these trends, but to trade the intraday news announcement, you need to be nimble and have a direct-access trading platform. You should be prepared for very fast-paced price action and trade it accordingly. Web-based brokers generally don't have the order entry and order execution speeds that are needed to reliably trade the intraday FOMC moves. Although the length of an intraday FOMC move could last 5 to 10 minutes, it could also be over in a matter of seconds to just a few minutes. When trading the FOMC trend, I look for popular momentum stocks such as FB, AAPL, and Goldman Sachs (GS). The truest way to play this trend is with DIA, SPY, or QQQ, the index ETFs. Figure 13.8 is a chart of the FOMC moves, using the Dow Jones Industrial Average ETF (DIA) as the example.

You can see the initial spike was a biggie, followed by a decent-sized pullback and then ultimately the market just rip-roared into the close. We caught this move in the Legends of Wall Street trading room (affinitytrading.com) where I had called the market *green* when it was down about 150 points. Figure 13.9 is a chart of FB during the same time frame; you can see the direct correlation to the DIA chart.

If I'm picking a momentum stock, I want stocks that tend to move with the market, and, preferably, outperform the market. If you prefer to lower your overall risk exposure rather than trading an individual stock, you can just take one of the index ETFs.

The January Effect

The January effect trend is another strong trend that has worked every year but one or two since I've been tracking it. The January effect is a well-known and widely followed trend. It is similar to the window-dressing trend. In fact, you might think of it as a form of year-end window dressing. Once again, fund managers don't want to show stocks on their books that have done poorly during the year, so they frequently sell them at some point during the last quarter of the year. Other factors contributing to the January effect include tax-loss selling, new money coming into the market at the beginning of the following year, and funds buying back their favorite beaten-down stocks, especially since they are now more attractively priced as a result of the year-end selling. You'll often see very large percentage gains as a result of the January effect.

Timing the Trade

Generally, though sometimes it may be earlier or later, the stocks that have sold off earlier in the quarter will start a January effect run about the twentieth of December. Once again, you don't want to hold January effect stocks long term into the New Year. January effect

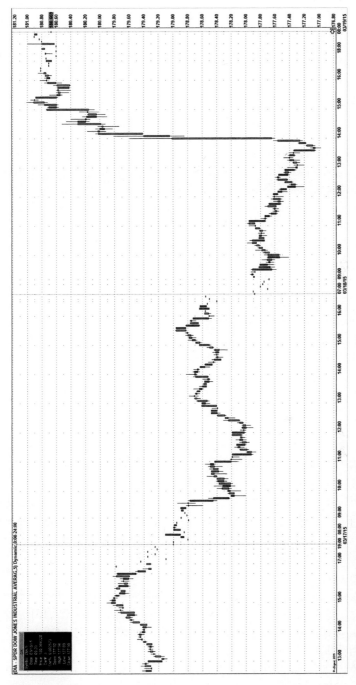

Figure 13.8 FOMC Chart DIA FOMC Date on March 18, 2015

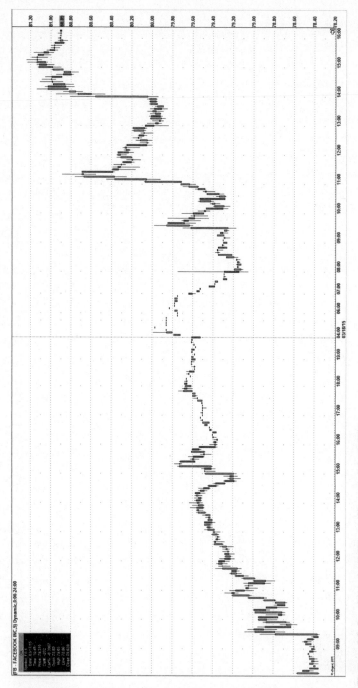

Figure 13.9 Chart of FB on March 18, 2015

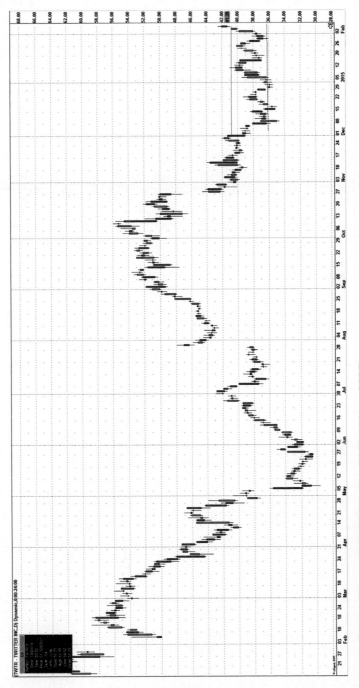

Figure 13.10 Chart of TWTR for Dec. 2014/Jan. 2015

stocks tend to start selling off about the fifth day of the New Year as a general rule. By this time, the bulk of new money and prior sellers are in the market so the buying pressure begins to wane. I like to play stocks that have sold off but have not yet bounced back significantly. Though the actual stocks I pick each year vary depending on market conditions and the price action of individual stocks, recent examples of stocks we have played for the January effect in 2014–2015 include Market Vectors Oil Services ETF (OIH), TWTR, and Go Pro (GPRO) (see TWTR chart in Figure 13.10).

Additionally, I look for small-cap opportunities. I like to trade the January effect using options as well. Not only does it let me precisely define my risk, but also I can often achieve even bigger percentage gains. In some cases, I've achieved gains in the hundreds of percent using options. Some of my clients who played the trend using options have made hundreds of percent, or even thousands (yes, 1000s) on the trade. The stocks subsequently often give back all of their gains during the first part of the New Year, serving as an example of why you don't want to hold a stock more than a few days into the New Year. I've seen the January effect impact many other stocks essentially the same as shown in this example. While I will occasionally go short to trade the downside move of a January effect play during the first week of January, it is always subject to specific market conditions and the potential risk/reward of a trade. Generally, shorting the downside move isn't as reliable as trading the upside move.

CHAPTER

14

Finding Your Own Animal Spirit

Ah, the penultimate question. How do *you* find your own favorite strategies, your own winning formula? What *animal spirit* do you embody?

I hope that by now you have even a small inkling of what appeals to you enough for you to take it to the next step.

Next Steps

If that's the case, and you feel like one, or even a half-dozen ideas I've discussed, appeal to you, then great, you are well on your way to putting together your own trading business plan! Or, conversely, it's fine if you read this book and decide, "Hey, these ideas aren't for me." That's totally cool as well. Cool isn't a technical analysis term, just an FYI. My point is that I tell clients and I'll tell you the same thing: Just because this works for me, doesn't mean that it's *right* for you. I've found that when it comes to career, there are rarely *wrong* and *right* answers. There are so many variables that go into why someone decides to do what they ultimately do, it would take a few books to cover. This is about personal choice, appeal, and what's realistic. A few years ago, my youngest daughter was diagnosed with type 1 diabetes and some other challenges. I could no longer trade the way I had been used to. The change was so drastic that I had a very hard time adjusting, and I lost a *lot* of money. I blew my account up, I floundered; I was a lost puppy. I decided I would become even more of a teacher than I had been; my priorities changed. I obviously didn't want the changes I was getting, but as a single dad with sole custody of my then-eight-year-old daughter, it's not like I had a whole helluva lot of choices. And, that's okay; life gives us lemons; we can choose to suck on them, or make pizza out of them, right? Yes, I know we can choose to make lemonade, but too many clichés get boring, and since my daughter is a diabetic, we don't drink much lemonade anyway!

Choices

What we did do, though, is we started the framework for what I hope by 2016 or 2017 becomes a real business for my daughters. We started Emma and Joelle's Sweet Hearts, which is a sugar/gluten/nut–free dessert business. The site should be done by the time you read this, so stop by and say hi and order some great *healthy* desserts—www .ejsweethearts.com. Regardless, we took a negative and turned it as positive as we could.

Perhaps you are not yet ready to trade full time, or you just don't want to do that. Okay, so that takes some of the trends discussed here out of the equation, right? You can't power trade all day if you work full time as well. So, that narrows your scope quite a bit. Then you ask yourself how much time do you *want* to spend trading, *then* you ask how much time can you spend trading.

I like to try to turn everything into *choices*, rather than problems, or somehow acting as if we are victims. So, try to think about this as a *choice*. Yes, you may have three kids and a dog to feed, so getting rid of your steady job isn't a realistic (or smart) option to start, so if you *want* to trade full time, you can't right now. But, it's a choice *you* are making.

Laws of Attraction

According to the laws of attraction we have the power to control our destinies through and by focusing on positive or negative thoughts. By concentrating on positive thoughts, we can bring about positive results. Conversely, by focusing on negative thoughts we will attract negative outcomes. Like attracts like the same way like energy attracts like energy in the universe. Think about what happens when you go to the mail expecting to see bills and are stressed. Chances are, that's exactly what you'll find. Try thinking about positives and perhaps you'll end up with a few more checks that come your way!

Now, the skeptics will tell you that there is no scientific data to back this theory up. For me, however, I know firsthand that it does *work*. Doesn't mean nothing bad happens to you if you have a positive attitude, but the way you handle it can be as positive as possible. People still get old and die, my daughter Emma still has juvie diabetes, but the way we cope and the way we heal is very much in our control. One of the best days of my life was when Emma, who has struggled *mightily* with this horrible disease, said to me, without prompt—"Daddy, I'm not happy I have diabetes, but since I do have it, I'm happy I understand what it's like to have a disease so that now I can help others who struggle, too."

You obviously don't know my baby girl, but suffice to say those words would have never come out of her mouth a year, or two, or three ago—ever. She had to come to a place where she is ready to make a choice about how she deals with it.

We are force-fed so many negatives in our society. We turn on the TV, or our smartphone, and what do we see? The news is filled with practically all negatives. About the best the news does is tell you if your team won. Everything else is about what's wrong with the world, and what we should currently fear.

Fear is often (not always) *false evidence appearing real.* Yeah, you should fear walking down a dark alleyway where three people got mugged. That's *healthy* fear, but oftentimes we all, I think, have fear about things that aren't real. We fear financial ruin (been there many times), we fear a spouse will leave (*oy vey,* have I been there), we fear our kids will get sick, and sometimes they do—we can and do fear many, many things. I'll tell you, though, for me, I only do well in the present moment. I don't do well in the future, and I can't fix or change my past. It's called the *present* for a reason—it's usually a gift!

I once heard Paul Newman, the actor and philanthropist, in an interview. The question was, "How did you get to be Paul Newman?"

Newman's reply was brilliant, beautiful, and quite inspiring. He said, "I just accepted the gifts that were offered to me."

Think about how pure that is, and real. How many times in your life have you been offered something, or someone, and you turned it away out of fear? Fear of the unknown, fear of the safety and false security you might lose? Most of us, if we're honest, have turned away many gifts. I grew up in a really, really horrible setting. I was taught to fear *everything,* and what I didn't fear I was taught to feel guilty about. So, when a girl I liked liked me, well, I didn't like me, so I usually rejected her. It's the old Woody Allen joke, "I wouldn't want to belong to any club that would have me as a member."

Even when I got successful trading, I could have easily been a *lot* more successful, but I had a hard time accepting the gifts. I made lots of financial mistakes, and the crazy thing is, at my peak money-wise, I had more fear about being homeless again than I had ever had before. It probably sounds odd, or nutty, but trust me, it's true. I couldn't sleep because I was so worried I would eventually end up on the streets. Hey, maybe I will. Life turns in many ways, but living with that fear caused me to lose a lot of money trading out of desperation, something we obviously try not to do. I had no reason to be desperate, but as a kid I was desperate, and old fears are hard to overcome.

It took me many years to finally see that fear for what it is. Many successful people experience washouts, or blow themselves up financially until they figure out that it doesn't serve them. Maybe you have had that experience.

It's *all okay!* That's what I'm here to tell you. It's all good, as long as we learn from it and do things differently if we need to make changes. And, the choices you make about trading, about your home life, your work elsewhere, your relationships—these are all lessons that, if we allow them to be, are invaluable.

Are You a Leopard?

I have met hundreds of thousands of people from around the world because of my trading career. I don't think anything is set in stone, but I do think making changes in one's life and the way we go about it can be incredibly challenging. Some people just can't change their spots. It's why the recidivism rate for convicts is so high. You need a ton of strength to make core changes. You have to wake up each day and really get that this is your chance to be a "new" you. I don't know about you, but every morning when I take a shower, I feel *new*. It's amazing how such a simple, basic thing we get to thankfully do in our society (that *billions* of others don't get to do!) can have such a profound influence on the way I view and go about my day. *You* have to make choices to succeed in order to succeed.

I can't tell you how many clients I've had over the years who tell me how they "never win" or they "always pick the wrong play." My retort? If you keep telling yourself that, it'll be a self-fulfilling prophecy, I can promise you that. I can't promise you'll be successful as a trader, but I can promise you that if you do certain things, you will fail. Of that I'm sure.

CHAPTER 15

Zen and the Art of Rich

Have you ever thought about what truly defines *success* to you? Before you give a knee-jerk reaction, I'd like to ask you to do a 15-minute writing project. I'd like you to literally take a few sheets of paper—don't use your computer please—and write for at least 15 minutes what *success* means to you. There's no right or wrong answer, you won't get graded, and no one will see it unless you decide to share it.

It's important to write for at least 15 minutes because typically for the first 5 minutes people write something like this from their head, and not their heart. They write what the "right" thing is, the politically correct thing—"Being a good dad or mom; having friends who love me," and so on. Or, they write, "Being a billionaire and being able to fly my private jet around." Neither is right, neither is wrong. Maybe both are right or wrong for *you*.

Since no one is going to read this but *you*, the goal is to get you to be painstakingly honest. We're not looking to judge you, or for you to feel badly about whatever your truth is. We're just looking for an honest assessment of what your inner core believes is success for *you!*

Society

In our society many of us spend a lot of time judging or being judged, yet we often spend very little time doing self-inventories to really define ourselves, who we are, what we stand for, and what we want to be. How we want to act in the world is important. If you are like me, I believe we define who we are by how we react to any given person or circumstance. The tougher the challenge, the more our true selves are tested.

I believe we all start out as perfect beings and then we get all kinds of "stuff" and "baggage," both good and bad, heaped upon us. We inherit many of our parents' and relatives' belief systems, or if we have a troubled childhood, perhaps we revolt against their systems and do the opposite. Usually, it's a combo of both. I grew up in a pretty gosh-darn abusive setting. I don't need to get into the specifics here; I'll save that for my autobiography. Suffice it to say, I went to a trauma rehab for six weeks and was told by the woman who started it that in her more than 25 years working with trauma victims, my story was right up there with the worst she ever knew. That's not something to be proud of, it just "is what it is." I didn't choose that, the same way if you were born into a religious cult you didn't choose that.

But, at some point in our lives, we have to make choices that become our own, our true selves, as I like to call it. Or, we can simply lock ourselves up and live in denial; that's an unconscious choice, but it's a choice nonetheless.

Control ...

... is an illusion. We think we can control a lot of things in our lives, but I've learned from my own experiences we actually have *very* little control. As a kid, I couldn't control what my parents did or didn't do, nor could I control any adults at the two children's wards I lived at for two years from ages seven to nine. I prayed to G-d every day for help as I was tortured in any and all ways you could possibly think of. None came. As an adult, I went through a horrific seven-plus-year custody battle where I was yelled at, put down, threatened, and financially broken. Before that started, I was under the illusion that I had financial security, that I had enough money for me and my kids to live a very "rich" life. But, after seven years of paying my attorney millions and being sued by her attorney for his fees, I was basically bankrupt. I "won," as my attorney kept pointing out. I had sole custody of my youngest daughter, but I certainly didn't *win*.

And, when Emma was diagnosed with type 1 diabetes, and also various other issues, if I didn't learn how little true control I have, I certainly did then.

However, one of the main points of this book, I hope, is that there are things that we do have control of, and that aren't an illusion. All we can do as traders, or investors, is set ourselves up to be in the right place at the right time. We can set up trades that make sense, that have a logic behind them, and we can put them into play. Ultimately, we don't have control over the outcome, but we believe through experience that if we make the "right" trade, if we've done our homework and we aren't just willy-nilly closing our eyes and pointing, or throwing a dart at the wall to pick our trades and investments, more often than not, we will win, and in winning we can gain a foothold on securing our financial freedom! That's all we can do, and that's all I ask you to do.

Our advantage is in picking our spots—the minute we give up that advantage, we give up the control we do have. Taking "shots" isn't a viable financial strategy; it's gambling. And, the thing is, even in gambling there are smarter ways to play than others.

Ever play poker? The good players get all their money in the pot knowing that the odds are favorable, or often very favorable. Maybe you have two aces and the dealer just laid down another ace. That would seem like a good time to go all-in. And it's still a likely win, even if your opponent shows a jack, ten. Good poker players will made the right play, win or lose—and sometimes they do lose, just as sometimes we make the right trade and we lose. If the dealer turns over a queen, you'll sweat a little; if the dealer next turns a king, your beautiful hand just went down in flames. In poker, they call it a *bad beat*—the odds looked really good for your hand to be the best, and then the dealer turned over the only card that could have given your opponent the win. Again, the only control we have is that we made the right move, not in the results. Playing your aces is still the best move, even if the other guy sometimes gets lucky. We have to let go of the results and keep playing the right way. While there are never any guarantees, history gives us a good indication that over the long haul, we'll come out ahead, hopefully way ahead!

Money

I grew up very poor for the most part. My father left when I was two years old, and I've never seen him since. By all accounts, he was a miserable dude, beat me as a baby, and was physically abusive to my mother. He not only abandoned me, he also abandoned my newborn brother. He wasn't a deadbeat dad; he definitely doesn't deserve the word *dad* or *father* anywhere near his name. He was a deadbeat; he left my then-20-year-old mother to fend for herself. Didn't pay a nickel of child support, didn't do a thing. We lived in squalor. Food stamps, welfare, and my mother worked two or three jobs. She worked as a house cleaner and babysitter, often leaving me alone at three and four years old to care for my baby brother. If nothing else, my mother did what she needed to do for herself, my brother, Rory, and me to survive, and I will always respect, admire, and appreciate that about her.

This taught me a lot about money, and it also taught me a lot about what it means to be a good father and to show up for my own kids. Sometimes the best lessons in life are the hardest to go through. Viktor Frankl, in my favorite book, *Man's Search for Meaning,* stated that we learn our most-needed lessons through suffering. I like who I am. I'm a generous person, and I like that about myself. I learned that through the hardships I faced as a kid, and the ones I've faced as an adult as well.

Money can be a wonderful gift, or a destructive weapon. I hope that this book helps you achieve your financial freedom, or at least continues your journey toward it. Once you get there (which, if you work hard and are disciplined I believe most of you can), the test will be how you want to treat others—and money itself. Does it consume you? Or, is it the valuable tool that allows you to be a better person, a charitable person—something that enhances your ability to care for your family and others?

I've said it many times: I've been poor and miserable and poor and happy, and I've been rich and miserable and rich and happy. I prefer being rich and happy, but given the choice between being rich and miserable and poor and happy, I'd gladly take being poor and happy. Money can indeed buy you many things, but it doesn't buy you happiness or love, as the cliché goes. It's a tool that you can use to better your life, and that's what I hope you end up doing with the money I believe you are on a path to earning.

Cockroaches

I've told this story many times; I think it sums up a lot about my mother and my childhood. We lived at the time in the basement of a house. My mother paid $155 a month in rent, and we still couldn't pay it. My mother was behind a month on rent and the landlord threatened to evict us. One day, my mother came home from working all day and found me covered head to toe in cockroaches. She rushed me to the hospital because my body had broken out into hives all over. The next day, my mother took a cigar box with her as she knocked on the landlord's door. She handed the box to him and she told him—here is your rent. She turned and left. He opened the cigar box and found 155 roaches she had collected.

For my mother, at that point in her and our lives, success was survival. She succeeded against great odds, and in spite of the fact she battled her own inner demons.

Integrity

So, what else do we have control over? How we treat others and how we react in any particular situation. Our integrity. No one can take that away from us, it's our choice. Sometimes it's a hard choice, and none of us are perfect. I'm certainly not. The good and sometimes crappy thing about it is that those of us who aren't sociopaths and have consciousness never truly escape the thoughts when we know we've done something wrong. Having a sense of right and wrong, we do always know, ya know? Science has proven that we remember things most vividly when our adrenaline is cookin'. The most dramatic and traumatic things get etched in our memory; other things like where we put our keys, or when did I put the pizza in the oven, those things we forget easily (particularly when we get older). I remember the day I told Wendy K. that she was flat-chested…in sixth grade…and she kicked me in my most precious and delicate parts of my anatomy. I remember when my biological father left. I was two years old and he handed me a Teddy bear and said he'd see me soon. When we feel guilty, or scared, or angry, it triggers a biological response and it's hard not to remember those things—even when we don't want to.

My mother gave me many things; one of them was the gift and horror of *guilt*. I'm the guy who feels guilty for things I didn't even do! Growing up, she'd tell me she suffered for 18 hours during labor before I came out. I'm sure she didn't realize it when she would tell me that, but it made me feel guilty for anytime she was feeling sad or upset. There were times I felt guilty for breathing! So, at least for me, the best and easiest life path is to be as open and honest as humanly possible, cause when I'm not it haunts me. Hey, even when

I am (which is the very large majority of the time, thankfully) I can be haunted by it. *But,* I know one thing for certain, if I maintain my integrity, no one can take that away from me—except me. No matter how hard a situation appears, doing the right thing will, as clichés go—set you free ultimately!

Zen

So, what does any of this have to do with trading? Actually—a *lot!* I've found that the vast majority of my success in trading, and in life, happens when I don't even think about it, when I let go of the results. If you ask a poker player, a successful one, if he feels badly when he gets a "bad beat," he is likely to tell you, "Yeah, it sucks, but I'd make the same play every single time." As traders, all we can do is make the "right" trade. We make the *Zen* trade, and part of doing that is making a good, well-thought-out decision. As I've talked about throughout this book—the results are not in our control *other than*—plan your trade and trade your plan! I've found if I do that, I'll end up a winner more often than not in the long run. In the short run, yeah, I'll have my ups and downs. I try to be a big-picture person who stays in the moment. That's my Zen. Going with the flow of the universe is so important for us humans. It really is. Life throws us lots of curveballs. I don't care how much money you have, or don't have. I don't care how healthy we are this second—none of it matters at any given time. I had a really, really, hard childhood, but I'm an adult now, and while I can't control a lot, as I stated, I can control the decisions I make moment to moment, and most poignant, I can be the person I want to be no matter what happens.

One of the things that has helped me heal from my childhood trauma—and what great healers like Pia Mellody, John Bradshaw, and even someone like Viktor Frankl taught—was forgiveness. When I was growing up, I was very angry, and I carried that anger with me throughout some of my adult life. I hated my biological father for abandoning me and my brother and mother. I hated the people who molested and tortured me, or simply turned a blind eye and pretended it was okay to do these inhuman things to a child—me and many others where I was. And, that hatred consumed me. I wanted them all to die horrible deaths, and I spent time thinking about revenge or simply feeling sorry for myself. I sat on the pity pot for a long time. I drank, did drugs, did whatever I could to escape the pain I was in.

And, you know what? It only started to go away, I only started to heal, and I only started to *succeed* in various areas of my life, including my trading and financially, when I started to forgive them, and understand that my best "revenge" was my best success. All that time I spent hating and wishing it never happened, all it did was feed the beast. And, that beast certainly didn't help me; it simply kept me institutionalized, it kept me from creating my own destiny. I had to heal by forgiving my perpetrators, and instead of trying to understand why things happened, to look at the bigger picture. If I love myself and am kind to myself, then it doesn't matter why things happened, or why they will happen—it just matters that I look at the big picture, and that picture is of me as a good, honest man, a good father to my daughters, and a man among men and women who cares and is charitable. I can only be truly loving to others if I am truly loving to me.

Every minute, every hour, and every day we can start our lives over and be the person we yearn to be. We can choose how we treat others, and ourselves. We can walk in the world with our head held high, and light up any party we happen to attend. We can choose to make the right trades and take the right path to our financial freedom!

Choice is a wonderful thing, as long as we choose wisely. I hope you choose wisely and that this book provides you some insights that will help you on your most righteous and highest-self path!

CHAPTER 16

What Animal Spirit Are You?

So, now that we have talked about different trends, strategies, money management, bulls and bears, and other animals, the time has finally come for you to decide what *animal spirit* you are/aspire to be.

This is from a poem by the Netsilik Eskimos, called "Magic Words":

> In the very earliest time,
> when both people and animals lived on earth,
> a person could become an animal if he wanted to
> and an animal could become a human being.
> Sometimes they were people
> and sometimes animals
> and there was no difference.
> All spoke the same language.

Could you be the cougar, and embody wisdom without ego? The elephant who removes obstacles and barriers and represents patience and quiet confidence? Or, the eagle who is swift and strong, with courage and keen sight and insight? Who illuminates the spirit?

We've done some of the work necessary to find our trader selves—most of it to define who we think we are, or currently are. Now is the time to decide who you want to be. Now is the time for you to create your own destiny as a trader and human being.

Are you going to follow the laws of attraction and despite the doubts you may have, despite the losses of the past—you are going to decide to succeed?

And, if you are already successful, are you going to *decide to succeed and achieve greater heights?*

If you are able to accept responsibility for who you are and what you want to be—how you want to be in this world—then you are ready to be a successful trader, or find a path where you will be your best self.

Whatever your choices are, always remember that you weren't put on this planet to fail. Failure is an illusion if you look at failures as our greatest and most important life lessons.

We all fall off the proverbial horse, despite it symbolizing passion and personal drive and despite it being one of the few animals that can either be tame or roam free. We all fall, it's part of life—there is nothing we can do about it—the question is, do you get up and ride again, or are you defeated? Does the hungry lion continue to hunt bison even when he is outrun several times? If he wants to eat, he will. And, before you say, "Yes, but the lioness is the one who actually hunts, the lion is the protector," when lions are first sent out from their pride they have to learn to hunt on their own ... or die.

As a trader, you are on your own—you will either learn to hunt, or starve. By reading this book you are learning to hunt for yourself. When you start to put some of the teachings to work, the challenges will come and in the end you will fail, survive, or thrive based on how you handle adversity.

It is your positive attitude, your ability to weather the storm and appreciate it as the lesson it is, that will dictate your success.

Don't just succeed my friend. *Thrive.*

You have control over who you are and how you handle your life. You may be a great animal spirit at heart, but you are a human being, after all.

Peace, love, and light to all—may you find your path and be your highest self, achieving your highest purpose in all.

About the Author

Michael has been featured on CNBC; FOX News; FOX Business; Reuters; *Good Day, NY*; and in the *New York Times; Wall Street Journal; Financial Times; New York Post; Crain's Business*; and many others. His first book, *Rule the Freakin' Markets* (New York: St. Martin's Press, 2004), was an international bestseller and was published in six languages. He also authored *Rule Your Freakin' Retirement* (New York: St. Martin's Press, 2010) and *Power Trading/Power Living* (Houston: Ultimate Publishing, 2006).

Michael's had over 50 productions of his plays in New York City and California, and has produced six feature films; his first screenplay, *Random Acts of Kindness*, was a two-time finalist for the Sundance Film Institute's Writer/Director Labs and was later optioned by Dennis Hopper; he wrote and directed his first feature film, *Crazy for Love*, in 2005, and it won 14 festival awards, including four Best Feature awards and played in over 35 festivals around the world. Michael's life story was optioned by Dustin Hoffman, and he was honored at the United Nations for his charity work with abused children. Michael is the very proud father of Joelle and Emma Grace, his two amazing daughters.

Index